100 THINGS YOU SHOULD KNOW ABOUT COMMUNISM

SERIES:

In The U.S.A.

And Religion

And Education

And Labor

And Government

And Spotlight on Spies

August 15, 1949

Prepared and released by the Committee on Un-American Activities, U.S. House of Representatives, Washington, D.C.

SECOND PRINTING
AUGUST 15, 1949

Committee on Un-American Activities
U. S. House of Representatives

John S. Wood, Georgia, *Chairman*

Francis E. Walter, *Pennsylvania*

Burr P. Harrison, *Virginia*

John McSweeney, *Ohio*

Morgan M. Moulder, *Missouri*

J. Parnell Thomas, *New Jersey*

Richard M. Nixon, *California*

Francis Case, *South Dakota*

Harold H. Velde, *Illinois*

Frank S. Tavenner, Jr., *Counsel*

Louis J. Russell, *Senior Investigator*

John W. Carrington, *Clerk of Committee*

Benjamin Mandel, *Director of Research*

100 THINGS YOU SHOULD KNOW ABOUT

COMMUNISM
IN THE U.S.A.

The first of a series on the Communist conspiracy and its influence in this country as a whole, on religion, on education, on labor and on our government

"No Communist, no matter how many votes he should secure in a national election, could, even if he would, become President of the present government. When a Communist heads the government of the United States—and that day will come just as surely as the sun rises— the government will not be a capitalist government but a Soviet government, and behind this government will stand the Red army to enforce the dictatorship of the proletariat."

Sworn statement of
WILLIAM Z. FOSTER
*Head of the Communist Party
in the United States*

100 Things You Should Know About Communism in the U. S. A.

Forty years ago, Communism was just a plot in the minds of a very few peculiar people.

Today, Communism is a world force governing millions of the human race and threatening to govern all of it.

Who are the Communists? How do they work? What do they want? What would they do to you?

For the past 10 years your committee has studied these and other questions and now some positive answers can be made.

Some answers will shock the citizen who has not examined Communism closely. Most answers will infuriate the Communists.

These answers are given in five booklets, as follows:

1. One Hundred Things You Should Know About Communism in the U. S. A.
2. One Hundred Things You Should Know About Communism and Religion.
3. One Hundred Things You Should Know About Communism and Education.
4. One Hundred Things You Should Know About Communism and Labor.
5. One Hundred Things You Should Know About Communism and Government.

These booklets are intended to help you know a Communist when you hear him speak and when you see him work.

If you ever find yourself in open debate with a Communist the facts here given can be used to destroy his arguments completely and expose him as he is for all to see.

Every citizen owes himself and his family the truth about Communism because the world today is faced with a single choice: To go Communist or not to go Communist. Here are the facts.

1. What is Communism?

A system by which one small group seeks to rule the world.

2. *Has any nation ever gone Communist in a free election?*

No.

3. *Then how do the Communists try to get control?*

Legally or illegally, any way they can. Communism's first big victory was through bloody revolution. Every one since has been by military conquest, or internal corruption, or the threat of these.

CONSPIRACY is the basic method of Communism in countries it is trying to capture.

IRON FORCE is the basic method of Communism in countries it has already captured.

4. *What would happen if Communism should come into power in this country?*

Our capital would move from Washington to Moscow. Every man, woman, and child would come under Communist discipline.

5. *Would I be better off than I am now?*

No. And the next 17 answers show why.

6. *Could I belong to a union?*

Under Communism, all labor unions are run by the Government and the Communists run the Government. Unions couldn't help you get higher pay, shorter hours or better working conditions.

They would only be used by the Communists to help keep you down.

More complete details are given in ONE HUNDRED THINGS YOU SHOULD KNOW ABOUT COMMUNISM AND LABOR.

7. *Could I change my job?*

No, you would work where you are told, at what you are told, for wages fixed by the Government.

8. *Could I go to school?*

You could go to the kind of school the Communists tell you to, AND NOWHERE ELSE. You could go as long as they let you AND NO LONGER.

You could read ONLY what the Communists let you; hear only what they let you, and as far as they could manage, you would KNOW only what they let you.

For details, see ONE HUNDRED THINGS YOU SHOULD KNOW ABOUT COMMUNISM AND EDUCATION.

9. Could I belong to the Elks, Rotary, or the American Legion?

No. William Z. Foster, the head of the Communists in the United States, says:

Under the dictatorship all the capitalist parties—Republican, Democratic, Progressive, Socialist, etc.—will be liquidated, the Communist Party functioning alone as the Party of the toiling masses.

Likewise will be dissolved, all other organizations that are political props of the bourgeois rule, including chambers of commerce, employers' associations, Rotary Clubs, American Legion, YMCA, and such fraternal orders as the Masons, Odd Fellows, Elks, Knights of Columbus, etc.

10. Could I own my own farm?

No. Under Communism, the land is the property of the Government, and the Government is run by the Communists.

You would farm the land under orders and you could not make any decisions as to when or where you would sell the produce of your work, or for how much.

11. Could I own my own home?

No. Under Communism, all real estate in the city as well as the country belongs to the government, which is in turn run by the Communists.

Your living quarters would be assigned to you, and you would pay rent as ordered.

12. What would happen to my insurance?

The Communists would take it over.

13. What would happen to my bank account?

All above a small sum would be confiscated. The rest would be controlled for you.

14. Could I leave any property to my family when I die?

No, because you wouldn't have any to leave.

15. *Could I travel around the country as I please?*

No. You would have to get police permission for every move you make, if you could get it.

16. *Could I belong to a church?*

In Russia, the Communists have for thirty years tried every way they could to destroy religion.

Having failed that, they are now trying to USE religion from the inside and the same Party strategy is *now operating in the United States of America.*

See ONE HUNDRED THINGS YOU SHOULD KNOW ABOUT COMMUNISM AND RELIGION.

17. *Could I start up a business and hire people to work for me?*

To do so would be a crime for which you would be severely punished.

18. *Could I teach what I please with "academic freedom"?*

You would teach only what the Communists authorize you to teach. You would be asking for jail or death to try anything else.

19. *Could I do scientific research free of governmental interference and restrictions?*

Police and spies would watch your every move. You would be liquidated on the slightest suspicion of doing ANYTHING contrary to orders.

20. *Could I have friends of my own choice as I do now?*

No, except those approved by the Communists in charge of your life from cradle to grave.

21. *Could I travel abroad or marry a foreigner?*

You could do nothing of that sort except with permission of the Communists.

22. *Could I exchange letters with friends in other countries?*

With the police reading your mail, you could try—once.

23. *Could I vote the Communists out of control?*

No. See ONE HUNDRED THINGS YOU SHOULD KNOW ABOUT COMMUNISM AND GOVERNMENT, showing the facts of Communist government in other countries and the facts of Communism at work within OUR OWN government.

24. But doesn't Communism promise poor people a better life?

Communist politicians all over the world try in every way to break down nations as they are, hoping that in the confusion they will be able to seize control.

Promising more than you can deliver is an old trick in the history of the human race.

Compare Communism's promises with Communism's performances in countries where it has come to power.

25. What are some differences between Communist promise and Communist performance?

When it is agitating for power, Communism promises more money for less work and security against war and poverty.

In practice, it has not delivered any of this, anywhere in the world.

26. But don't the Communists promise an end to racial and religious intolerance?

Yes, but in practice they have murdered millions for being religious and for belonging to a particular class. Your race would be no help to you under Communism.

Your beliefs could get you killed.

27. Why shouldn't I turn Communist?

You know what the United States is like today. If you want it exactly the opposite, you *should* turn Communist.

But before you do, remember you will lose your independence, your property, and your freedom of mind.

You will gain only a risky membership in a conspiracy which is ruthless, godless, and crushing upon all except a very few at the top.

28. How many Communists are there in the world?

There are 20,000,000 Communists, more or less, in a world of 2,295,125,000 people. In other words, about one person in 115 is a Communist, on a world basis.

29. How many people are now ruled by Communism?

About 200,000,000 directly; 200,000,000 more indirectly, and an additional 250,000,000 are under daily Communist pressure to surrender.

30. Which countries are Communist controlled or governed?

Albania, Bulgaria, Czechoslovakia, Estonia, Finland, Hungary, Latvia, Lithuania, Poland, Romania, Russia, Yugoslavia.

Important regions of Austria, Germany, Korea, Mongolia and Manchuria.

Communism is concentrating now on immediate capture of Afghanistan, China, France, Greece, Latin America, Iran and Palestine.

It has plans to seize every other country including the United States.

31. How many Communists are there in the United States?

There are approximately 80,000 out of a population of 145,340,000 people. J. Edgar Hoover has testified that "in 1917 when the Communists overthrew the Russian Government there was one Communist for every 2,277 persons in Russia. In the United States today there is one Communist for every 1,814 persons in the country."

32. Why aren't there more?

Because the Communist Party does not rely upon actual Party membership for its strength. J. Edgar Hoover testified:

"What is important is the claim of the Communists themselves that for every Party member there are ten others ready, willing, and able to do the Party's work. Herein lies the greatest menace of Communism.

"For these are the people who infiltrate and corrupt various spheres of American life. So rather than the size of the Communist Party the way to weigh its true importance is by testing its influence, its ability to infiltrate."

33. How are they organized?

Primarily around something they call a political party, behind which they operate a carefully trained force of spies, revolutionaries, and conspirators.

The basic fact to remember is that Communism is a world revolutionary movement and Communists are disciplined agents, operating under a plan of war.

34. Where are their headquarters in the United States, and who is in charge?

Headquarters are at 35 East Twelfth Street, New York City. William Z. Foster, of 1040 Melton Avenue, New York City, has the title of "Chairman of the Communist Party of the United States," but Foster is actually just a figurehead under control of foreign operatives unseen by and unknown to rank and file Communists.

35. What is the emblem of the Communist Party in the United States?

The hammer and sickle.

36. What is the emblem of the Communist Party in the Soviet Union?

The hammer and sickle.
It is also the official emblem of the Soviet Government.

37. What is the flag of the Communist Party in the United States?

The *red flag*, the same as that of all Communist Parties of the world.

38. What is the official song of the Communist Party of the United States?

The Internationale. Here is the Chorus:

> *'Tis the final conflict,*
> *Let each stand in his place;*
> *The International Soviet shall be the human race.*

39. Do the Communists pledge allegiance to the flag of the United States?

The present head of the Communists in the United States has testified under oath that they DO NOT.

40. What is the Communist Party set-up?

At the bottom level are "shop and street units" composed of three or more Communists in a single factory, office, or neighborhood.

Next is the section which includes all units in a given area of a city. Then come districts, composed of one or more States.

At the top is the national organization, composed of a national committee and a number of commissions.

11

In the appendix of this pamphlet you will find listed the officers and address for each district of the Communist Party in the United States.

41. Who can become a member of the Communist Party of the United States?

Anybody over 17 years of age who can convince the Party that his first loyalty will be to the Soviet Union and that he is able to do the Party's work as a Soviet agent.

He must be an active member of a Party unit. He must obey ALL Party decisions. He must read the Party literature. He must pay dues regularly.

42. How do you go about joining the Party?

You must know some member in good standing who will vouch for you to his Party unit. Your acceptance still depends on the verdict of Party officials that you WILL AND CAN obey orders.

43. Can you be a secret member?

All Communists are secret members until authorized by the Party to reveal their connection. Party membership records are kept in code. Communists have a real name and a "Party name."

44. Are meetings public like those of ordinary political parties?

No, meetings are secret and at secret addresses. Records are all secret and in code. Public demonstrations are held at regular periods.

45. What dues do you have to pay?

They are adjusted according to income. They may range from as low as 2 cents a week to $15 a week with special assessments in addition.

46. What do you have to promise?

To carry out Communist Party orders promptly. To submit without question to Party decisions and discipline.

To work for "The triumph of Soviet power in the United States."

47. After you join, what do you have to do?

You have to obey the Party in all things. It may tell you to change your home, your job, your husband, or wife. It may order you to lie, steal, rob, or to go out into the street and fight.

It claims the power to tell you what to think and what to do every day of your life.

When you become a Communist, you become a revolutionary agent under a discipline more strict than the United States Army, Navy, Marines, or Air Force have ever known.

48. Why do people become Communists then?

Basically, because they seek power and recognize the opportunities that Communism offers the unscrupulous.

But no matter *why* a particular person becomes a Communist, every member of the Party must be regarded the same way, as one seeking to overthrow the Government of the United States.

49. What kind of people become Communists?

The real center of power in Communism is within the professional classes.

Of course, a few poor people respond to the Communist claim that it is a "working class movement."

But taken as a whole the Party depends for its strength on the support it gets from teachers, preachers, actors, writers, union officials, doctors, lawyers, editors, businessmen, and even from millionaires.

50. Can you quit being a Communist when you want to?

The Communists regard themselves as being in a state of actual war against life as the majority of Americans want it.

Therefore, Party members who quit or fail to obey orders are looked on as traitors to the "class war" and they may expect to suffer accordingly when and as the Party gets around to them.

51. How does the Communist Party of the United States work, day by day?

The Communist Party of the United States works inside the law and the Constitution, and outside the law and the Constitution with intent to get control any way it can.

52. What are some types of Communist activities within the law?

Working their way into key positions in the schools, the churches, the labor unions, and farm organizations. Inserting Communist propaganda into art, literature, and entertainment. Nominating or seeking control of candidates for public office. The immediate objective of the Communist Party is to confuse and divide the majority so that in a time of chaos they can seize control.

53. What are some types of Communist activities outside the law?

Spying, sabotage, passport fraud, perjury, counterfeiting, rioting, disloyalty in the Army, Navy and Air Force.

54. What are some official newspapers or magazines of the Communist Party?

Daily and Sunday Worker, 50 East Thirteenth Street, New York City; Morning Freiheit, 50 East Thirteenth Street, New York City; Daily Peoples World, 590 Folsom Street, San Francisco, Calif.; Masses and Mainstream, 832 Broadway, New York City; Political Affairs, 832 Broadway, New York City. There are also numerous foreign language publications.

55. Does the Party also publish books and pamphlets?

Yes, thousands of them, through such official publishing houses as: International Publishers, 381 Fourth Street, New York City; Workers Library Publishers, 832 Broadway, New York City; New Century Publishers, 832 Broadway, New York City.

56. Does the Party have public speakers and press agents?

Hundreds of them, paid and unpaid, public and secret, hired and volunteered, intentional and unintentional.

Publicity seeking is one of the Party's principal "legal" occupations, intended to confuse people on all important issues of the day.

57. How does the Party get the money for all this?

At first it received money from Moscow but now it raises millions of dollars here in the United States through dues, foundations, endowments, special drives, and appeals.

58. Do only Communists carry out Communist work?

No. The Party uses what it calls *"Fellow Travelers"* and *"Front Organizations"* in some of its most effective work.

59. *What is a fellow traveler?*

One who sympathizes with the Party's aims and serves the Party's purposes in one or more respects without actually holding a Party card.

60. *Is he important in the Communist movement?*

Vital. The fellow traveler is the **HOOK** with which the Party reaches out for funds and respectability and the **WEDGE** that it drives between people who try to move against it.

61. *What is a Communist front?*

An organization created or captured by the Communists to do the Party's work in special fields. The front organization is Communism's greatest weapon in this country today and takes it places it could never go otherwise—among people who would never willingly act as Party agents.

It is usually found hiding among groups devoted to idealistic activities. Here are 10 examples out of hundreds of Communist fronts which have been exposed:

1. American Committee for Protection of Foreign Born.
2. American Slav Congress. .
3. American Youth for Democracy.
4. Civil Rights Congress.
5. Congress of American Women.
6. Council for Pan-American Democracy.
7. International Workers Order.
8. National Committee to Win the Peace.
9. People's Institute of Applied Religion.
10. League of American Writers.

62. *How can a Communist be identified?*

It is easy. Ask him to name ten things wrong with the United States. Then ask him to name two things wrong with Russia.

His answers will show him up even to a child.

Communists will denounce the President of the United States but *they will never denounce Stalin.*

63. *How can a fellow traveler be identified?*

Apply the same test as above and watch him defend Communists and Communism.

64. How can a Communist front be identified?

If you are ever in doubt, write the House Committee on Un-American Activities, Room 226, House Office Building, Washington 25, D. C.

65. What do Communists call those who criticize them?

"Red baiters," "witch hunters," "Fascists." These are just three out of a tremendous stock of abusive labels Communists attempt to smear on anybody who challenges them.

66. How do they smear labor opposition?

As "scabs," "finks," "company stooges," and "labor spies."

67. How do they smear public officials?

As "reactionaries," "Wall Street tools," "Hitlerites," and "imperialists."

68. What is their favorite escape when challenged on a point of fact?

To accuse you of "dragging in a red herring," a distortion of an old folk saying that originally described the way to throw hounds off the track of a hot trail.

69. What is the difference in fact between a Communist and a Fascist?

None worth noticing.

70. How do Communists get control of organizations in which the majority are not Communists?

They work. *Others won't.*
They come early and stay late. *Others don't.*
They know how to run a meeting. *Others don't.*
They demand the floor. *Others won't.*

They do not hesitate to use physical violence or ANY form of persecution. They stay organized and prepared in advance of each meeting. The thing to remember is that Communists are trained agents under rigid discipline, but they can always be defeated by the facts.

71. When was the Communist Party of the United States organized, and where?

September 1919, at Chicago.

72. Has it always been called by its present name?

No. Here are the recorded, official name changes:

1919—Communist Party of America, and the Communist Labor Party of America.

1921—The above parties merged into the United Communist Party of America.

1922—The Communist Party of America and the Workers Party of America.

1925—The above merged into one organization known as Workers (Communist) Party of America.

1928—Communist Party of the United States.

1944—Communist Political Association.

1945 to present—Communist Party of the United States of America.

73. Why has it changed its name so often?

To serve Moscow and evade the law of the United States.

74. Why isn't the Communist Party a political party just like the Democratic and Republican parties?

Because it takes its orders from Moscow.

75. Are the Communists agents of a foreign power?

Yes. For full details write the Committee on Un-American Activities, Room 226, House Office Building, Washington 25, D. C., for House Report No. 209, entitled The Communist Party of the United States as an Agent of a Foreign Power.

76. Where can a Communist be found in everyday American life?

Look for him in your school, your labor union, your church, or your civic club. Communists themselves say that they can be found "on almost any conceivable battlefront for the human mind."

77. What States have barred the Communist Party from the ballot?

Alabama, Arkansas, Illinois, Kansas, Ohio, Oklahoma, Oregon, Tennessee, and Wisconsin.[1]

---

[1] This list was compiled as of January 1948.

78. How does Communism expect to get power over the United States if it cannot win elections?

The Communists only compete for votes to cover their fifth-column work behind a cloak of legality. They expect to get power by ANY means, just so they get it.

The examples of Poland, Czechoslovakia, and other countries in Europe show just how many methods Communism applies.

In each country different details—in all the same result.

79. Why don't Communists over here go to Russia if they like that system so much?

They are on duty here to take over this country. They couldn't go to Russia even if they wanted to, except on orders from Moscow.

80. Which Communists get such orders?

High Party officials and special agents who are to be trained in spying, sabotage, and detailed planning for capture of this country.

81. Where are they trained in Moscow?

The Lenin Institute, a college in revolution which teaches how to capture railroads, ships, radio stations, banks, telephone exchanges, newspapers, waterworks, power plants, and such things.

82. Does Stalin let American Communists in to see him?

Yes. Earl Browder and William Z. Foster, the two heads of the Party for the last 20 years, have both admitted under oath that they conferred with Stalin.

The records show that Browder, for instance, made 15 known trips to Moscow, several with false passports.

83. Are American Communists used in the Soviet Secret Service?

Yes, here are the names of a few such agents proved on the public records:

Nicholas Dozenberg, George Mink, Philip Aronberg, Charles Dirba, Pascal Cosgrove, J. Mindel, Alexander Trachtenberg, Julia Stuart Poyntz, Jack Johnstone, Charles Krumbein, and Albert Feirabend.

84. What central organization controls all the Communist Parties of the world?

An organization originally set up in Moscow by the Government of Russia, and known as the "Communist International" called *Comintern* for short.

It has since changed its name to "Communist Information Bureau" and is known as the *Cominform*.

85. *Who is the most important Communist in the United States today?*

The *Cominform* representative.

86. *Why is he here?*

To see that American Communists follow the orders of the Soviet-directed *Cominform* in all things.

87. *Do they?*

Yes.

88. *Has any representative of this central organization ever been caught?*

Yes. For example, over a period of 12 years one Gerhart Eisler, alias Brown, alias Edwards, alias Berger, did such work, making regular trips between the United States and Europe.

On February 6, 1947, his activities were exposed by the House Committee on Un-American Activities and he has since been convicted in court of perjury and contempt of Congress.[2]

89. *What is the best way to combat Communism?*

Detection, exposure, and prosecution.

90. *Are these being done?*

Millions of dollars have been spent by the Federal Bureau of Investigation, Army and Navy Intelligence, and other executive agencies to detect and keep track of Communists since the Party's organization in this country a generation ago.

Exposure in a systematic way began with the formation of the House Committee on Un-American Activities, May 26, 1938.

Prosecution of Communists, as such, has never taken place in this country, as yet.

---

[2] Eisler jumped his bond of $23,000 and fled to Europe on the Polish liner *Batory* on May 6, 1949.

91. Have any Communists been prosecuted on other grounds?

Yes. For violations of such laws as those governing passports, immigration, perjury, criminal syndicalism, and contempt.

92. Is this enough?

No. The House of Representatives maintains this Committee on Un-American Activities to study the problems of Communism and all other subversive movements and recommend new laws if it feels they are needed.

93. Has the Committee made any such recommendations?

Yes. The latest is H. R. 5852, known as the Mundt-Nixon bill, which passed the House of Representatives on May 19, 1948, by a vote of 319 to 58.

94. What does this bill do?

The main points are:

To expose Communists and their fronts by requiring them to register publicly with the Attorney General and plainly label all their propaganda as their own.

To forbid Communists passports or Government jobs.

To make it illegal for ANYBODY to try to set up in this country a totalitarian dictatorship having ANY connection with a foreign power.

95. What is Communism's greatest strength?

Its secret appeal to the lust for power. Some people have a natural urge to dominate others in all things.

Communism invites them to try.

The money, hard work, conspiracy, and violence that go into Communism, add up to a powerful force moving in a straight line toward control of the world.

96. What is Communism's greatest weakness?

The very things that give it strength. For just as some people have a natural lust to dominate everybody else, so do most people have a natural determination to be free.

Communism can dominate only by force.

Communism can be stopped by driving every Communist out of the place where he can capture power.

97. What is treason?

Our Constitution says that "Treason against the United States, shall consist only in levying War against them, or in adhering to their Enemies, giving them Aid and Comfort. No Person shall be convicted of Treason unless on the Testimony of two Witnesses to the same overt Act, or on Confession in open Court."

98. Are the Communists committing treason today?

The Soviet Union has launched what has been called a "cold war" on the United States. Therefore, Communists are engaged in what might be called *"COLD WAR TREASON."*

The Mundt-Nixon bill is intended to fight this "cold war treason."

If our war with Communism should ever change from "cold" to "hot" we can expect the Communists of the United States to fight against the flag of this country openly.

99. What should I do about all this?

Know the facts. Stay on the alert. Work as hard against the Communists as they work against you.

100. Where can I get information about Communism regularly?

Write the House Committee on Un-American Activities, Room 226, Old House Office Building, Washington, D. C., for information regarding official publications.

APPENDIX

Principal officers and offices of the Communist Party, U. S. A., as of 1947.

COMMUNIST PARTY, UNITED STATES OF AMERICA

National headquarters: 35 East Twelfth Street, New York, N. Y.

Chairman—William Z. Foster.
General secretary—Eugene Dennis (Waldron).
Administrative secretary—John Williamson.
Treasurer—Vacant since the death of Charles Krumbein.
National secretariat:

William Z. Foster.
Eugene Dennis.
Robert Thompson.
John Williamson.
Benjamin J. Davis, Jr.
John Gates.
Gil Green.
Gus Hall.
Irving Potash.
Jack Stachel.
Carl Winter.
Henry Winston.

National committee:

William Z. Foster.
Benjamin J. Davis, Jr.
Rose Gaulden.
Mickey Lima.
John Williamson.
Nat Ganley.
Bella Dodd.
James Jackson.
Louis Weinstock.
William McKie.
Nat Ross (South).
Fred Blair.
Jack Stachel.
Gus Hall.
Nat Cohen.
Ferdinand Smith.
Abner Berry.
Alexander Bittleman.
Claudia Jones.
Alexander Trachtenberg.
David Davis.
Herb Signer.
Irving Potash.
Max Weiss.
Lem Harris.
Hal Simon.

National review board:
Chairman—Ray Hansborough.
Vice chairman—Vacant since the death of Charles Krumbein.
Secretary—Saul Wellman.
William McKie.
National labor commission:
Chairman—John Williamson.
Secretary—William Albertson.
Administrative secretary—Robert Minor.
Al Blumberg.
Pat Toohey.

National women's commission:

    Chairman—Elizabeth Gurley Flynn.

    Assistant secretary—Claudia Jones.

National Negro commission:

    Chairman—Josh Lawrence.

    Secretary—Henry Winston.

National group commission: Chairman—Steve Nelson.

National farm commission:

    Chairman—Max Weiss.

    Secretary—Lem Harris.

Organizing commission:

    Secretary—Henry Winston.

    Assistant Secretary—Betty Gannett.

Coordinating Committee, National Maritime Field—Al Lannon.

Jewish Commission:

    Secretary—Moses Miller.

    General Secretary—Alexander Bittleman.

Veterans' commission:

Director—John Gates.	Leon Straus.
George Blake.	Robert Thompson.
Joseph Clark.	Carl Vedro.
Louis Diskin.	George Watt.
Irving Goff.	Saul Wellman.
Howard Johnson.	Herbert Wheeldin.
Herbert Kurzer.	Henry Winston.
Carl Reinstein.	

Student's commission: Director—Marion Shaw.

Legislative commission:

    Chairman—Arnold Johnson.

    Secretary—Robert Minor.

Educational Agit-Prop., and publicity commission:

    Chairman—Jack Stachel.

    Secretary—Max Weiss.

DISTRICT AND LOCAL OFFICIALS

Northeast district, 80 Boylston Street, Boston, Mass.

(States included: Massachusetts, Maine, New Hampshire, Rhode Island, Vermont)

Chairman (district)—(Manny) Emanuel Blum.

Secretary (district)—Fanny Hartman.

Chairman (Massachusetts section)—Otis A. Hood.

    Committee members for Massachusetts:

        Jack Green.

        Hy Gordon (trade union secretary, Massachusetts).

William E. Harrison.

Arthur E. Timpson (husband of Anna Durlak).

Joseph C. Figueiredo (Bristol organizer).

Organizer, Boston—F. Collier.

Secretary-treasurer (district)—Hugo Gregory.

Educational director, Massachusetts—Alice Gordon.

State (Massachusetts) campaign committee—Frances Hood (Mrs. Archer Hood).

Chairman, New Hampshire section—Elba Chase Nelson.

Labor secretary and Massachusetts organizer—Daniel Boone Schirmer.

Chairman (Maine)—Lewis Gordon.

Eastern Pennsylvania-Delaware district, 250 South Broad Street, Philadelphia, Pa.

(States included: Eastern Pennsylvania and Delaware)

Chairman (district)—Phil Bart.

Secretary (district)—Bob Klonsky.

Committee members:

Tom Nabried.	Bill McKane.
Estelle Shohen.	Jessie Schneiderman.
Carl Reeve.	Sam Donchin.
Jules Abercaugh.	John Devine.

Secretary, thirty-sixth ward (Philadelphia)—Bill Brockman.

Financial secretary (district)—Ben Weiss.

Organizer, Wilkes-Barre section—Joseph Dougher.

Organizer (district)—Sam Rosen.

Member, labor committee—David Davis.

Western Pennsylvania district, 417 Grant Street, Pittsburgh, Pa.

(Western Pennsylvania)

Chairman—Roy Hudson.

Secretary—Dave Grant.

Organizer—J. G. Eddy.

Chairman, Lawrenceville section—Matt Cortich.

Organizer, Lawrenceville section—Eleanor Sackter.

Organizer, Jones & Laughlin Club of Communist Party (Pittsburgh)—Sam Reed.

Youth organizer, Pittsburgh—Mike Hanusik.

Executive secretary (district)—Peter Edward Karpa.

Committee members:

Joe Godfrey.	Ben Careathers.
Elmer Kish.	Gabor Kist.
Dave Grant.	

Maryland-District of Columbia district, 210 West Franklin Street, Baltimore, Md., and 527 Ninth Street NW., Washington, D. C.

(Maryland and Washington, D. C.)

Chairman (district)—Phil Frankfeld.
Secretary (district)—Dorothy Blumberg.
Chairman (District of Columbia section)—William Taylor.
Vice chairman (District of Columbia section)—William S. Johnson.
Secretary (District of Columbia section)—Elizabeth Searle.
Treasurer (District of Columbia section)—Mary Stalcup.
Literary director (District of Columbia section)—Casey Gurewitz.
Cumberland organizer—Mel Fiske.
Director, membership committee—Constance Jackson.

District of Ohio, 2056 East Fourth Street, Cleveland, Ohio

(State of Ohio)

Chairman—Gus Hall.
Secretary—Martin Chancey.
Organizing secretary—Frieda Katz.
Organizer—A. Krchmarek.
  Committee members:

Gus Hall.	Carl Guilood.
Abe Lewis.	Elmer Fehlhaber.
Edward Chaka.	Martin Chancey.
Bernard Marks.	Mike Davidow.
Robert Hamilton.	

Chairman, Cedar-Central section—Abe Lewis.
Chairman, Cuyahoga County section—Gus Hall.
Chairman, Cleveland County section—Elmer Fehlhaber.
Secretary, Cleveland County section—Mike Davidow.
Organizer, Toledo section—Nat Cohn.
Organizer, Cincinnati section—Robert Gunkel.
Organizer, Akron section—Bernard Marks.

Minnesota, North Dakota, and South Dakota district, 1216 Nicollet Street, Minneapolis, Minn.

(States included: Minnesota, North Dakota, and South Dakota)

Chairman (district)—Martin Mackie (Minnesota).
Secretary (district)—Carl Ross.
Assistant secretary (district)—Rose Tillotson.
Chairman, Hennepin County section (Minnesota)—Robert J. Kelly.
Secretary, Pine County, Minn., district—Clara Jorgensen.

District of Indiana, 29 South Delaware Avenue, Indianapolis, Ind.

(State of Indiana)

Chairman—Elmer Johnson.
Secretary—Henry Aron.
Legislative director, Indiana and Illinois—William Patterson.
 Committee members:

Elmer Johnson.	Benjamin Cohen.
Morris Porterfield.	Imogene Johnson.
Sylira Aron.	

District of Michigan, 902 Lawyers Building, Detroit, Mich.

(State of Michigan)

Chairman—Carl Winter.
Secretary—Helen Allison.
National committee representative—James Jackson.
Educational director—Abner Berry.
Youth director—Robert Cummings.
Daily Worker representative—Mabel Mitchell.
Organizer—Fred Williams.
 Committee members:

Hugo Beiswenger.	Joe Brandt.
Geneva Olmsted.	

Chairman, Ypsilanti, Willow Run section—Thomas Dennis.
Chairman, Flint section—Thomas Kelly.
Chairman, Hamtramck section—Thomas Dombrowski.
Secretary, New Haven—Joseph Gonzales, Jr.
State literature director—Byron Edwards.
Chairman, Flint—Berry Blossinghame.
Chairman, Michigan Avenue, Detroit section—John Hell.

District of Illinois, 208 North Wells, Chicago, Ill.

(States included: Illinois and Kentucky)

Chairman, Illinois section—Alfred Wagenknecht.
Chairman (district)—Gil Green.
Vice Chairman—William L. Patterson.
Assistant secretary—Victoria Kramer.
Legislative director, Illinois section—Edward Starr.
Labor secretary, Illinois section—Fred Fine.
Chairman, East Side Chicago section—Claude Lightfoot.
Section organizer—Jim Keller.
Organizer—Henry Davis.
Section organizer, Ninth Congressional District—Ethel Shapiro.
Organizer, South Chicago section—James Balanoff, Jr.

Chairman, twenty-eighth ward—Sylvia Woods.
Chairman, third ward—Ishmael Flory.

District of New York, 35 East Twelfth Street, New York, N. Y.

(State of New York)

Chairman—Robert Thompson.
Vice chairman—Rose Gaulden.
Organizing secretary—William Norman.
Organizer—Donald MacKenzie Lester.
Director of education—William Weinstone.
Secretary of education—Sam Coleman.
Legislative director—Bella Dodd.
Farm organizer—George Cook.
Youth director—Lou Diskin.
Secretary, legislative committee—Lillian Gates.
Director, industrial section—Ben Gold.
Chairman, Negro committee—Charles Lohman.
Director, veterans' committee—John Gates.
Assistant director, veterans' committee—Howard Johnson.
Director, Daily Worker veterans' committee—Joe Clark.
Assistant organizational director—Charles Lohman.
Chairman, Communist Party Club, New York City—Leon Beverley.
Water front organizers—Tom Christensen and Al Rothbart.
Italian section organizer—Antonio Lombardo.
State secretariat:

Robert Thompson.	Israel Amter.
Hal Simon.	William Norman.

Committee members (in addition to above):

Nat Slutsky (section organizer).	Elwood Dean.
Michael Salerno.	George Watt.

Harlem section:
Chairman—Benjamin J. Davis, Jr.
Executive secretary—Robert Campbell.
Administrative secretary—John Lavin.
Industrial section director—Rose Gaulden.
Organizing director—Anselo Cruz.
Organizing secretary—Bonita Williams.
Educational director—Carl Dorfman.
Committee members:

Bob Campbell.	Carmen Lopez.
Bonita Williams.	Horace Marshall.
Rose Gaulden.	Benjamin J. Davis, Jr.
Larry Washington.	Sam Patterson.
Leon Love.	Maude White.

Cyril Phillips.
Fern Owens.
Theodore Bassett.
John Lavin.

Letty Cohen.
Herb Whiteman.
Oscar James.

New York County section:
Executive secretary—George Blake Charney.
Membership director—Clara Lester.
Educational director—Rebecca Grecht.
Executive committee members:

James Tormey.
Louis Mitchell.
Howard Johnson.
Esther Cantor.
Tom Christensen.

Robert Campbell.
Ester Letz.
David Greene.
Evelyn Wiener.
Alvin Warren.

Queens County section:
Chairman—Paul Crosbie.
Organizer—Dave Rosenberg.
Secretary—James A. Burke.
Educational director—Helen Stuart.
Organizing secretary—Fay Collar.
Sectional organizer—Milton Goldstein.

Bronx section:
Chairman—Isidora Begun.
Organizing secretary—Bob Appel.
Press director—Bob Alpert.
Educational director—Robert Klonsky.
Assistant educational director—Henry Kuntzler.

King's County section:
Chairman, women's committee—Margaret Cowl (Krumbein).
Sectional organizer—Carl Vedro.
Press director—Mickey Langbert.

Essex County section: Chairman—Martha Stone.

Manhattan County section:
Executive secretary—George Charney.
Press director (industrial)—Al Reger.

Brooklyn section: Organizing secretary—John White.

Miscellaneous sections:
Chairman, Buffalo—Lloyd Kinsey.
Organizer, Buffalo—Nicholas Kosanovich.
Assistant to chairman, Buffalo—Norman Ross.
Chairman, Rochester—Gertrude Kowal.
Chairman, Syracuse—George Sheldrick.
Chairman, Utica—Murray Savage.
Chairman, Schenectady—Harold Klein.
Chairman, Binghamton—Irving Weissman.

Chairman, Yonkers—Edna Fried.
Chairman, Astoria, Long Island—Esther Signer.
Secretary, Nassau County—John Lavin.
Secretary, Coney Island—William Albertson.
Organizing secretary, eastern New York—Morris Smith.
Director, Nassau County—Jim Faber.
Chairman, Melrose—Joe Jackson.
Literature director, Middletown—Rose Walsh.
Organizing secretary, Williamsburg—Leon Nelson.
Organizer, Brownsville—Abe Osheroff.
Organizer, Nassau—Sam Faber.
Chairman, Westchester—Herbert L. Wheeldin.
Section organizer—Leon Nelson.
Press director, Bright Beach—Harry Klein.
Organizer, Morrisania—Morris Stillman.
Organizer, Allerton—Bernard Schuldiner.
Organizer, Parkchester—Sparky Friedman.
Organizer, Jamaica—Charles Evans.

Northwest district, 1016½ Second Avenue, Seattle, Wash., and 916 East Hawthorne Street, Portland, Oreg.

(States included: Idaho, Oregon and Washington)

Chairman (district)—Henry Huff.
Labor secretary (district)—Andre Remes.
Secretary Pierce County section—Clara Sear.
Director, People's World, Seattle—Marx Blashko.
Committee members (in addition to above):

C. Van Lydegraf.	Edward Alexander.
Barbara Hartle.	

Chairman, Spokane section—William L. Cumming.
Chairman, Oregon section—Ead Payne.
Secretary, Oregon section—Mark Haller.

District of California, 942 Market Street, San Francisco, Calif.

(State of California)

Chairman—William Schneiderman.
Organizing secretary—Loretta Starvis.
State treasurer—Anita Whitney.
State field organizer—Mickey Lima.
State educational director—Celeste Strack.
People's Daily World circulation director—Leo Baroway.
Chairman youth commission—George Kaye.
Chairman, Jewish commission—A. Olken.
State press director—Ida Rothstein.
State youth director—George Kaye.

Labor secretaries—Archie Brown and Leon Kaplan.

Committee members:

John Pittman.	Loretta Starvis.
Louise Todd.	Nemmy Sparks.
Ray Thompson.	Clarence Tobey.
William Schneiderman.	George Lohr.
Pettis Perry.	Mickey Lima.

State political editor—Douglas Ward.

Secretary, water-front section—Herbert Nugent.

Los Angeles County section:

Chairman—Nemmy Sparks.

Labor secretary—Ben Dobbs.

Press director—Elizabeth Ricardo.

Chairman, minorities commission—Pettis Perry.

Organizing secretary—Dorothy Healy.

Editor, People's Daily World—Sidney Burke.

Chairman Sixteenth Congressional District—Emil Freed.

Section organizer—Alvin Averbuck.

Legislative director—Harry Daniels.

Harbor section organizer—Jim Forrest.

Veterans' director—Merel Brodsky.

Youth director—Phil Bock.

Secretary, Carver Club section—Mort Newman.

Candidate, board of education—La Rue McCormack.

Candidate, councilman—Henry Steinberg—Ninth District.

Candidate, councilman—James C. McGowan—Eleventh District.

Candidate, councilman—Elsie M. Monjar—Eighth District.

Director, West Adams Club of Communist Party—Joe Klein.

Social activity secretary, 62 AD, Communist Party—Ida Elliott.

Northern California section:

Chairman, San Francisco section—Oleta Yates.

Legislative director, San Francisco section—Herb Nugent.

Labor director, San Francisco—Leon Kaplan.

Water-front organizer—Alex Freskin.

Educational director, San Francisco—Aubrey Grossman.

San Diego County section: Chairman—Enos J. Baker.

Alameda County section:

Chairman—Lloyd Lehman.

Labor director—Wesley Bodkin.

Organizer, Ben Davis Club of Communist Party (Alameda)—Buddy Green.

Trade-union director, Hariet Tubman Club of Communist Party (Alameda)—Helen Bodkin.

Miscellaneous section:

President, Santa Monica Club of Communist Party—David Grant.

Chairman, Contra Costa County—Mildred Bowen.

Chairman, Hollywood section—John Stapp.
Press director, East Side Youth Club (Los Angeles)—Libby Wilson.
Organizer, North Oakland section—George Edwards.

District of Arizona, 716½ North Washington Street, Phoenix, Ariz.

(State of Arizona)

Chairman—Morris Graham.
Committee members:
  Lewis Johnson.
  Karl M. Wilson.
Chairman, Maricopa County—M. Dallen.

District of New Jersey, 38 Park Place, Newark, N. J.

(State of New Jersey)

Chairman—Sid Stein.
Organizing secretary—Larry Mahon.
Section organizer, Plainfield—Al Muniz.
Committee members:
  Martha Stone (Scherer).
  Tom Scanlon.
  Irving Glassman.
  Joseph Magliaco.
  Elwood Dean.
  Mrs. Gaetana Mahan.

District of Connecticut, 231 Fairfield Avenue, Bridgeport, Conn.

(State of Connecticut)

Chairman—Joe Roberts.
Secretary—Mike Russo.
Committee members (in addition to above):
  Rudolph Gillespie.
  Roy A. Leib.
Chairman, Hartford section—Roy A. Leib.
Chairman, New Haven section—Sidney S. Taylor.

District of Wisconsin, 617 North Second Street, Milwaukee, Wis.

(State of Wisconsin)

Chairman—Fred Blair.
Secretary—E. Eisenscher.
State committee—Sigmund Eisenscher.
Chairman, Milwaukee section—G. Eisenscher.
Chairman, sixth ward—Joe Ellis.
Secretary, Milwaukee section—Clarence Blair (alias Clark).
Organizer, Milwaukee—James Phillips.

District of Colorado, 929 Seventeenth Street, Denver, Colo.

(States included: Colorado, New Mexico, and Wyoming)

Chairman—William Dietrich.
Secretary—Arthur W. Barry.
Organizational secretary—Tracy Rogers.

District of Missouri, 1041 North Grand Street, St. Louis, Mo.

(State of Missouri)

Chairman—Ralph Shaw.
Secretary—Nathan Oser.

District of West Virginia, Charleston, W. Va.

(State of West Virginia)

Chairman—Ted Allen.

Southern District

(States included: Texas, Louisiana, Florida, Georgia, Virginia, Alabama, Mississippi, Tennessee, Oklahoma, North Carolina, and South Carolina)

Chairman, Texas—Ruth Koenig, 305 Herman Building, Houston, Tex.
Executive secretary, Texas—James J. Green.
Chairman, Houston section—William C. Crawford.
Chairman, Louisiana—James E. Jackson, Jr.,
Secretary, Louisiana—Kay Davis, Godchaux Building, New Orleans, La.
Chairman, Florida-Georgia—Alex W. Trainor, 1546 Loma, Jacksonville, Fla.
Organization secretary, Florida-Georgia—Homer Chase.
Chairman, Virginia—Alice Burke, 102 North Eighth, Richmond, Va.
Chairman, Alabama-Mississippi-Tennessee—Harold Bolton.
Secretary, Alabama-Mississippi-Tennessee—Andy Brown.
Press director, Alabama-Mississippi-Tennessee—Harry Raymond.
Organizer, Alabama-Mississippi-Tennessee—Mary Southard.
Chairman, Oklahoma—Allen Shaw.
District organizer, Oklahoma—H. Smith, Oklahoma City, Okla.
Organizing secretary, Oklahoma—Al Lowe.
Organizing secretary, North and South Carolina—Sam Hall.

District of Montana, 2117 Fourth Avenue South, Great Falls, Mont.

(State of Montana)

Chairman—Ira Siebrasse.

District of Nebraska, 415 Karback Building, Omaha, Nebr.

(State of Nebraska)

State chairman—Warren Batterson.

District of Utah, 75 Southwest Temple Street, Salt Lake City, Utah

(State of Utah)

State chairman—Wallace Talbot.
State secretary—Joseph Douglas.

100 THINGS YOU SHOULD KNOW ABOUT

COMMUNISM
and RELIGION

The second of a series on the Communist conspiracy and its
influence in this country as a whole, on religion, on
education, on labor, and on our government

94252°—49——5

J. EDGAR HOOVER:

"I confess to a real apprehension, so long as Communists are able to secure ministers of the gospel to promote their evil work and espouse a cause that is alien to the religion of Christ and Judaism."

EARL BROWDER:

". . . we Communists do not distinguish between good and bad religions, because we think they are all bad . . ."

100 THINGS YOU SHOULD KNOW ABOUT COMMUNISM AND RELIGION

This is to tell you what will happen to *YOU* and *YOUR CHURCH* if Communism ever takes over the United States of America.

The long and the short of it is just this: You cannot be a Communist and believe in God. You cannot believe in God and have a peaceable life under Communism.

In all their plans and actions, the Communists mark down religion as Enemy No. 1. Where they dominate, they attack it head on. Where they do not dominate, they try to deceive and to corrupt from within just as they do in government, in education, in labor unions, and throughout a nation's life in general.

The aim and object of Communism is always the same—complete control over the human mind and body, asleep and awake, in sickness and in health, from birth to death. That is why Communism marks religion Enemy No. 1, for religion in some form is always a basic influence in the life and thinking of any people.

Communism cannot dominate family life, for example, until it has first fought its way past the influence of religion upon the family.

Communism cannot force its own brand of moral code upon a person without first destroying his moral code rooted in religion.

Communism cannot make education a weapon in its hands so long as religion is secure in its own right to teach and to educate.

Communism cannot dominate unless it has the power to remake the life of the people. It cannot ignore religion and do that.

So here, then, is a report on what Communism seeks to do about religion in the U. S. A., as judged by what it has already done elsewhere and has *SAID* it will do here at the first opportunity:

1. If Communism should come to the United States, could I belong to a church?

You would have to choose at once between church and Communism. If you should choose the church, then prepare for persecution

2. What would the Communists DO to churches and synagogues?

Take them over and put an end to the freedom now guaranteed by Sentence One, Article One in the Bill of Rights of the Constitution:

> Congress shall make NO law respecting an establishment of religion or prohibiting the free exercise thereof.

3. What does that mean, exactly?

Just study for a minute these figures on the present size and nature of religion and its works in the U. S. A.:

> 256 denominations.
> 253,000 churches and synagogues.
> 77,000,000 members.
> 162,000 Sunday schools.
> 13,000 parochial schools.
> 690 colleges and schools of higher learning.
> Libraries, radio stations, publishing houses for books, magazines and newspapers.
> Charities, orphanages, hospitals, missionary forces.
> Ladies' aids and auxiliaries. Men's societies, young people's organizations, children's groups.

These are what Communism would like to take over and destroy.

4. Would the Communists destroy the Bible?

Every copy they could find. And they would jail anybody trying to print new copies.

5. Could I be married in the church?

Not legally.

6. Could my funeral be held in the church?

Not legally.

7. Could my child be baptized or christened in the church?

At the risk of prison for parent and pastor.

8. Would my child go to Sunday school?

Not only would Sunday school be illegal, but also your child would be taught to report you to the police for trying to send him.

9. *How would my child learn his religion, then?*

Only through what you might tell him at home, to offset the positive atheism he would learn all week at the government school.

10. *You mean the GOVERNMENT would teach atheism?*

Yes. Here is the rule laid down by Nikolai Lenin, leader of the Communist revolution in Russia in 1917 and founder of the Red government now headed by Joseph Stalin:

> Down with religion! Long live atheism! The spread of atheist views is our chief task!

That rule has not changed.

11. *Could I give money to the church?*

Yes, if the Communist system would allow you any; but then most of it would go for staggeringly high taxes, rent, and other fees charged by the government to discourage church operations. Anything left could go to feed the preacher, who would be little better off than a beggar, anyhow.

12. *Who would own the churches?*

Under Communism, churches and synagogues could no longer own their own property, free, clear, and untouchable, as they do in the United States today. Church property would become government property. Congregations could only use such small rooms or buildings as the government might license to them on concession.

The fees and charges for this would be heavy and all use would be subject to strict Communist control, review and supervision.

13. *How about my own church-going?*

You could try on your own time, if the Government happened at the time to let you off work on a holy day. Otherwise, only at night, when and if you got the chance.

14. *Would I be allowed time off for religious holidays and celebrations as now?*

Not a chance.

15. *Could I help out with church charities and welfare work?*

There wouldn't be any. All church schools, hospitals, orphanages, asylums, and such things would be seized by the government. Religion would be denied any say in their use or management.

16. What about missionary work?

Illegal. Forbidden.

17. Could we print the sermons, church notes or news letters?

Certainly not. Only atheistic views could be distributed and, of those, only such as the government would hand out in official form. Under Communism you wouldn't even be free to peddle your own brand of atheism—just the government's.

18. How about my church men's club, ladies' aid society, or young people's group?

Out. There is no freedom of assembly under Communism.

19. What could my pastor do?

In the pulpit, he could lead the congregation in acts of faith and deliver sermons, with the Communists checking on every word.

Out of the pulpit, he would be an official target for abuse, ridicule, and scorn, under constant suspicion, and in danger of his life.

20. Why?

In him, the Communists would see a rival to their power over your mind, imagination, and will. The faith your pastor teaches is Communism's deadliest enemy.

21. What do you mean by "faith"?

The sort of thing you find in the Ten Commandments and the Sermon on the Mount.

22. What is the COMMUNIST faith?

"Marxism-Leninism," as operated by Joseph Stalin.

23. What's all that?

A plan and method to rule the world.

The man who drew up the plan was Karl Marx, who lived from 1818 to 1883.

The man who put the plan into action in real life was Vladimir I. Ulyanov, alias Nikolai Lenin, who lived from 1870 to 1924, and led the world Communists to capture Russia in 1917–18.

The man who made the plan a world force was Josif Vissarionovich Djugushvili, alias Josif Stalin, now living, and 68 years old, who followed Lenin in command of the world Communist conspiracy.

24. Why do you say "alias Lenin" and "alias Stalin"?

Because those are not the real names of the men involved.

Remember, the present "Stalin" started out in life to destroy the government of his own country and rebuild it on Communist lines through bloody revolution, and that's how it was actually done.

He was against all law except Communist ideas as laid down by Karl Marx. He used the alias "Stalin" to hide his real identity, just as Ulyanov used "Lenin."

25. What was Marx' idea of a Communist world?

That the world as we know it must be destroyed—religion, family, laws, rights, everything. Anybody opposing was to be destroyed, too.

Marx wanted a world in which people owned no property, took orders from the Government without question, and let their family life—husbands, wives, parents, and children—be without religion, morals, or ideals as we know them.

26. What was his idea of morality and family?

That anything is moral—even lying, stealing, and murder—if it brings on Communism.

That women should have children for the Communist state to educate, train, and use, but parents should not have any say in training according to their OWN ideas.

That there is no need to fear God because He does not exist.

Marx had the idea that people could never be happy, have enough to eat, make enough money, or have success in the kind of world we know.

The U. S. A. is living proof that he was as wrong as a man can be.

27. Was Marx crazy?

Perhaps. But Marx was not the first evil and crazy man to start a terrible world upheaval, nor was he the last. Hitler was like that, too, but look at what he did.

28. How did anybody fall for Marx?

Some overlooked his craziness because he was one of the most effective propagandists who ever lived.

His preaching of destruction appealed especially to people who wanted to rule others and didn't know how. It still does.

29. Was Lenin one of those power seekers?

Yes. Lenin was the son of a minor Government clerk. He had a terrible thirst for power.

Early in his life he read Marx, caught the idea of forming Communist cells of revolution as Marx planned them, and built a conspiracy to capture his country.

When Russia's Czarist Government crashed in the war of 1914–18, it was followed by a Republic organized along the lines of our own. But before the Republic could really take hold, Lenin's Communists came out from under cover, confused the public mind by propaganda, stirred a military revolt, slaughtered all opposition and set up by force of arms a Communist dictatorship. They still have it today.

30. Did all the Russians turn Communist?

Neither then nor now. Only a few trained and disciplined favorites were or are allowed to be Communists.

For a general picture of what kind of people turn Communist and what they DO, see the first of this series, entitled "100 Things You Should Know About Communism in the U. S. A."

31. Why do any people fall for their line?

They promise all the things that people have always sought—an easier life, an end to trouble.

32. Do they deliver?

Of course not.

Once they get in control, they reduce a nation to horror and slavery. Look at the record, not only in Russia but in all other countries captured by Communism.

33. How do they keep going?

The secret of Communism's drive and the real key to the Communist faith is the dream of total power for Communists, loss of power for all others. That's the story in a nutshell.

34. Where is the headquarters of the Communist faith?

The Kremlin, Moscow, Russia.

35. Who is the head of that faith?

Joseph Stalin, because he is the head of the Government of Russia and Chief of the Communist Party of Russia. To a Communist in the United States or any other country, Stalin's word is final.

For a Communist to defy Stalin is as scandalous to other Communists as for a religious-minded person to blaspheme God.

36. *Is there any proof of this?*

Examine the record in Russia, Latvia, Lithuania, Estonia, Poland, Czechoslovakia, Hungary, Romania, Bulgaria, Yugoslavia, Austria, Germany, and in all other countries where Communism takes any hold.

Add to it the thousands of volumes of Communist official literature collected in the Library of Congress here in Washington.

Measure against your common sense and decide for yourself. In the meantime, here following are significant highlights from that record dealing with just one side of the story, Communism's war on religion all over the world, including the United States of America.

37. *What about Russia?*

Let's flash back. The number of congregations has dropped since 1917 by more than 75 percent. That any have remained at all is a triumph of survival against relentless, cruel, and powerful persecution.

38. *Was Russia a very religious country before?*

About half the people of the old Russian Empire belonged to the Eastern Orthodox branch of Christianity. The Orthodox Church was recognized and established as an arm of the Government.

Beyond the established church, there were congregations of Roman Catholics, Protestants, Jews, Mohammedans and other faiths, even ancient tribal pagan groups.

None beyond the Orthodox Church was recognized as legally "established" by the Government, but they were at least tolerated. They are not even TOLERATED now. Only the Orthodox sect is allowed any activity at all.

39. *Why is the Orthodox church an exception?*

Its priests are today held captive by the Communists and used to help rule the Russian people.

40. *How did the Communists capture them?*

By destroying the independent power of the church and then taking advantage of the determination of many people to have a continuing religious service on any terms.

41. What was the first step?

All Orthodox Church property, right down to the crucifixes and altar vessels, was seized. All monasteries closed. Churches turned into movie houses and museums. Church bells destroyed.

42. How were Orthodox priests treated?

Thousands were slaughtered. Others were ridiculed and kicked through the streets. As a class, they were held up to the country as parasites and frauds, and refused permission to travel, meet in groups, or to train or ordain others.

43. How about the other faiths?

Treated even worse, since they represented minority groups.

44. What else happened?

Official Government agencies were set up with the taxpayers' money to operate "antireligious museums" and to publish books, posters, pamphlets, and magazines denouncing religion. Atheist carnivals were held on religious holidays. Christmas trees were banned. Sunday was decreed a workday to stop devotional services, and failure to report for work on a religious day meant instant dismissal. Religious oaths were abolished.

Atheism was taught in the schools as a required course for all children. Radio broadcasts by Government propagandists dinned atheism into people's ears night and day. Communists who showed any interest in religion were expelled and ruined. Priests and their families were made outcasts of society, refused jobs or food-ration cards, and forced to pay extra rent and taxes.

Orthodox priests are allowed to marry, so the Government even took it out on their children by refusing them so much as a high school education.

Non-Communists who stood by their religion lost their jobs and generally were shoved downhill by the full force of government.

45. Was all this effective?

Figures on congregations and church organizations in Soviet Russia vary, but over-all they show a general reduction in church organizations of 75 to 90 percent over a 25-year period. The number of priests in the Russian Orthodox Church was reduced from nearly 51,000 down to less than 6,000. Orthodox Churches dropped from 46,000 before the Communists took over to 2,000 in 1948.

However, religion went underground as a result of persecution, and a vast network was created in which priests carried on religious schools and services in secrecy and survived in disguise with the help of the general public.

It has been estimated that today there are, in addition to the nearly 6,000 registered priests mentioned above, another 5,000 under cover; there are at least 2,000,000 children in underground Christian youth organizations; and there are between 67,000,000 and 80,000,000 adult believers in Russia.

46. Are the Communists satisfied with the damage accomplished so far?

No. They will never accept as final anything less than the complete end of religion.

47. Have the Russian Communists EVER tolerated religion?

They have **pretended** to on a few occasions when it served their purpose. While Communists do not have religion themselves, they have sometimes agreed that personal faith is all right so long as churches obey Communism's orders against missionary, welfare and charity work, and religious education of children.

48. Why is this?

The Russian Communists have needed cooperation from religious-minded people in their own country, and they also want religious people outside the borders of Russia to help the Communists there seize control of other countries. "Toleration" of religion is just a tactical maneuver in Communism's war on civilization. Long-range strategy of total destruction does not change.

49. When was this "toleration" tactic first used in Russia?

Although very minor concessions to the church were allowed in 1923 and 1935, after two of the most severe waves of religious persecution, the first significant pretense of religious tolerance came in 1938. A general order went out to "avoid jarring the religious sensibilities of the believers."

50. Why?

Because Stalin was afraid of Hitler's growing power and wanted the Russian people to be unified and cooperative in case of war.

When war did come, the Russian Communists used priests to appeal to the Russian people for support of the war. The Moscow radio actually called upon "God-loving inhabitants" of German-occupied countries to rise in defense of religious freedom. References to God were even found in Stalin's papers and addresses.

The Government also temporarily closed its atheistic publishing concerns as a war maneuver. Churches in Moscow took on a blaze of outward life.

51. Did this mean Stalin had lost his nerve as an atheist?

Not at all. He simply turned the church into a weapon for his own use on the home front then, and such it remains today.

52. Do the Communists pretend to tolerate religion today?

No. Since the end of World War II, the Russian Government has renewed open war against religion in all forms, although in some countries Communists pretend to tolerate it to serve their propaganda purposes.

53. How do we know this?

A recent statement in an official Soviet newspaper listed the stamping out of religious faith "by systematic, scientific, antireligious propaganda" as "the most important task in the struggle for the triumph of Communism in the U. S. S. R."

Communist Party members in Russia, both young and old, were publicly ordered recently to work against religious beliefs.

Radio Moscow is carrying atheistic broadcasts and hammering at the people with Marx' well-known words, "Religion is the opium of the people."

54. How do the Communists control the Orthodox Church?

Through the Soviet Government's State Council on Orthodox Affairs, headed by Georgi Karpov, an atheist Communist who for years had been a member of the Soviet Secret Police. Every decision of the church officers must be approved by Karpov, even down to the point of getting his permission to go on a trip.

44

55. How do Americans of the Russian Orthodox faith feel about the state of their faith in Russia?

Russian Orthodox bishops and priests here refuse to accept the Russian church any longer as a guide or source of religious authority.

56. Is the Roman Catholic Church restored in Russia?

In no way. One priest is allowed to stay in Moscow for the benefit of foreigners there, but the church is entirely shut off from the people of the country as a whole.

57. How about the Jews?

The same. Hebrew, the sacred language of the Judaic faith, is forbidden by law. Feast days, religious development and enjoyment for Jews have been suppressed as harshly as for any others.

58. How about Protestant groups?

They have been crushed.

59. What has Communism done against religion outside Russia?

It has seized church and synagogue property and killed church leaders wherever and whenever Communism has gained control.

Where it has not yet gained the upper hand over the country as a whole, it has tried to corrupt religion from within by setting sect against sect and creed against creed.

60. Are Communists trying to corrupt religion in the U. S. A.?

Yes.

61. What is their method?

The Communist Party of the United States assigns members to join churches and church organizations, in order to take control where possible, and in any case to influence thought and action toward Communist ends.

It forms "front organizations," designed to attract "fellow travelers" with religious interests.

It tries to get prominent religious leaders to support Communist policies, disguised as welfare work for minorities or oppressed groups. In the words of Earl Browder, former head of the Communist Party of the U. S. A.:

> ". . . By going among the religious masses, we are for the first time able to bring our anti-religious ideas to them."

62. What is a "front organization"?

An organization created or captured by the Communists to do the Party's work in special fields. The front organization is Communism's greatest weapon in this country and takes it among people who would never willingly act as Party agents.

63. What is a "fellow traveler"?

One who sympathizes with the Party's aims and serves the Party's purposes without actually holding a Party card.

64. How can I spot them?

Many organizations have been listed as Communist fronts by the Attorney General and this Committee. You can get a list of these by writing to the House Committee on Un-American Activities, Room 226, Old House Office Building, Washington, D. C.

To show up a fellow traveler, ask him to name ten things wrong with the United States and then ask him to name two things wrong with Russia. He will be on Russia's side every time.

65. Are American Communists atheistic?

Yes.

66. Can a Communist ever have religious beliefs?

When he first joins the Party, a Communist may still have some religious faith but it soon goes or he fails as a Communist.

67. What happens to a religious person who turns Communist?

The Party ridicules his religious ideals and dins atheist propaganda into his ears, day and night, in an attempt to convert him to atheism.

68. What if a new Communist refuses to renounce religion?

Kicked out.

69. What happens to a person who gets kicked out of the Party?

He is hounded for the rest of his life.

70. Have the Communists used blasphemous propaganda against the church?

If there is any doubt in your mind as to the vicious and blasphemous propaganda Communists are using against religion, then go to your public library and read a typical example of it entitled "Goodbye, Christ," by Langston Hughes.

It is so atrocious that we will not reproduce it here, but even so, it is mild compared to the atheist propaganda in Moscow.

71. How do Communists work among church people, since they themselves are such haters of religion?

Communists are two-faced.

In their secret Party meetings, they make plans to destroy religion.

In public, they say religion and Communism should be friends and that both are working for the same goals.

72. Are there Communist clergymen?

Unfortunately, yes.

73. Do they admit they are Communists?

Some do, but except in special cases, the Party requires Communists to keep their membership secret.

74. Will you give an example of the "open" type of membership?

The Rev. Claude C. Williams, a Presbyterian minister, whose congregation expelled him for Party activity. The Rev. Eliot White, retired Episcopalian minister, who served as a delegate to a Communist convention and lectured at Communist meetings.

75. Are they important?

Not as important as the others who have joined the Communist fronts which the Attorney General and this committee have declared to be "subversive."

76. Do you mean that just because a clergyman joins or sponsors one or two Communist fronts for one reason or another, he is playing Stalin's game in America?

No. We are talking about those clergymen who have over a period of years consistently followed the Party line and joined, not one or two fronts, but ten, twenty, or thirty. These are the core of agents the Party depends on in the religious field.

77. But couldn't some of these clergymen be innocently misguided in their attempts to do good?

Well, they have followed every crook and twist of the Communist Party line. Would you excuse that in your minister's case?

78. Is your Committee investigating religion?

Certainly not. Religion is not under any sort of investigation by the House Committee on Un-American Activities, nor is any sect, creed, church, or individual, so far as his religion is concerned.

79. Then what's this pamphlet for?

To help you protect your religion and faith from Communist attack by showing you exactly what the Communists are up to.

80. But is Communism a "real" danger inside our churches?

Here's J. Edgar Hoover on the subject:

> I confess to a real apprehension, so long as Communists are able to secure ministers of the gospel to promote their evil work and espouse a cause that is alien to the religion of Christ and Judaism.

81. Is Communist propaganda ever sneaked into church publications?

Yes. For instance, a minister was discharged as editor of an official church publication for permitting communistic propaganda to appear in this publication.

82. Do Communist propagandists ever actually get before church groups as speakers?

Yes. For example, the head of the Communist Party, on one occasion at least, spoke at Union Theological Seminary in New York City.

Only a few months ago, the Legislative Secretary of the Communist Party addressed a conference of 100 ministers in Washington, D. C.

83. What about church youth groups?

Young Communists are ordered to join them.

84. Why?

For two reasons: To win over youth to Communism and atheism, and to turn their groups into tools of the Communist Party.

85. Is this done openly?

No. Communist youth, like Communist adults, work under cover. They won't admit being Communists if you ask them unless and until their Party officers direct them to do so.

86. Is the YMCA a Communist target?

Yes. So is the YWCA.

Also, church youth groups.

87. Do you mean every youth group is a Communist hide-out?

Of course not. But we do mean that Communists *do* dig into such groups any way and any time they can.

We do mean they *have* dug into such groups, and are at it today.

We do mean that if you want to keep your own organization fit for your own family's membership, you had better stay on the alert.

88. How else do Communists spread atheism?

Indirectly in Communist schools such as the Jefferson School of Social Science in New York, and the California Labor School.

Also in the atheistic schools for children operated throughout the country by the International Workers Order.

89. What is the People's Institute of Applied Religion?

One of the most vicious Communist organizations ever set up in this country. Declared subversive by the Attorney General.

90. Where is it located and who are its officers?

4105½ Third Avenue, South, Birmingham, Alabama.

Rev. Claude C. Williams, director; Edna Joyce King, executive secretary; Owen H. Whitfield and Winifred L. Chappell, associate directors; Carl Haessler, Calla E. Tennant, and Clara M. Vincent, trustees; Cederic Belfrage, research director.

91. What does it do?

It teaches Communist ideas, pretending that they are Christian ideas.

92. What is the Methodist Federation for Social Action?

A tool of the Communist Party, denounced by numerous loyal American Methodists. It claims to speak for 17 Methodist Bishops and 4,000 clerics and laymen. Not an official church organization.

93. Where is it located and what is it trying to do?

150 Fifth Avenue, New York, New York. Although strictly unofficial as a "church" organization, it is trying to use the prestige of the Methodist Church to promote the line of the Communist Party.

94. What is "The Protestant"?

A magazine which fanatically spreads Communist propaganda under the guise of being a religious journal.

Its avowed purpose is to "build a bridge" between Christendom and Communism. Boasts support of 6,000 ministers but not actually connected with any official religious organization.

95. Where is it published and who are the officers?

It is published by Protestant Digest, Inc., at 521 5th Avenue, New York, New York. Editor: Kenneth Leslie; Associate Editors: James Luther Adams, John Hammond, Gerald Richardson.

96. Should such organizations have any church's support?

Ask your own pastor.

97. How can we combat them?

Reread this pamphlet. Show it to others. Become as interested in protecting your religion as the Communists are in destroying it.

98. Are the Communists just trying to get my church?

No. They're also out to get your job, to get your union, to get your farm, to get your school, to get your property, to get your Government. They're out to get YOU and make you a slave of Communism from cradle to grave.

If they can wreck your religion, that makes you just so much easier to capture and enslave.

99. When and how do they work on all these other angles?

See the other pamphlets in this series:

100 THINGS YOU SHOULD KNOW ABOUT COMMUNISM IN THE U. S. A.

100 THINGS YOU SHOULD KNOW ABOUT COMMUNISM AND LABOR.

100 THINGS YOU SHOULD KNOW ABOUT COMMUNISM AND EDUCATION.

100 THINGS YOU SHOULD KNOW ABOUT COMMUNISM AND GOVERNMENT.

100. Can the Communists win in all this?

It's up to you.

100 THINGS YOU SHOULD KNOW ABOUT

COMMUNISM

AND

EDUCATION

The third of a series on the Communist conspiracy and its
influence in this country as a whole, on religion, on
education, on labor, and on our government

*Give us the child for 8 years and
it will be a Bolshevik forever.*

—V. I. LENIN,
Founder of Communist Government in Russia

*Our teachers must write new school
textbooks and rewrite history
from the Marxian viewpoint.*

—WILLIAM Z. FOSTER,
Head of the Communist Party, U. S. A.

100 THINGS YOU SHOULD KNOW ABOUT COMMUNISM AND EDUCATION

This is to tell you what the master minds of Communism have planned for your child in the name of "Education."

They mean to take him from the nursery, put him in uniform with the hammer and sickle flag in one hand and a gun in the other, and send him out to conquer the world.

If they have their way, he will be guided from the kindergarten straight through to college so that he will have anything except a mind of his own.

He will be trained but not educated. He will be taught to solve problems that are handed him and to consider it a crime to think for himself. He will be the child-man of Communism.

Here are the facts in this, the third of a series on Communism:

1. What is Communism?

A conspiracy to conquer and rule the world by any means, legal or illegal, in peace or in war.

2. Is it aimed at me?

Right between your eyes.

3. What do the Communists want?

To rule your mind and your body from the cradle to the grave.

4. Are you joking?

Look at the world today and see if the people of Europe and Asia have anything to laugh about, now that Communism has captured so many of them.

5. If Communism should conquer America, what would happen to the schools?

Real education would stop. Only training would be allowed.

6. What's the difference?

All the difference there is between freedom and jail.

7. What is "education"?

People are "educated" when they learn to go after facts and to think for themselves.

8. What is "training"?

People are "trained" when they learn how to do a particular thing well and can be depended on to do it.

9. Which is better?

A monkey can be "trained" but only a human being can be "educated."

A man can very well improve himself by training in some specialty but only if he adds that training to independent thinking power, the hall-mark of education.

10. Are Communists really against education?

Yes, but don't take our word for it. Take theirs. The details here following are all from their own stuff.

11. What do they say?

Here's a quote from Lenin, founder of the Soviet state:

"Give us the child for 8 years and it will be a Bolshevik forever."

12. What's a "Bolshevik"?

The origin and history of that word tell a lot about Communism itself. The Russian word for "majority" is "bolshinstvo" and the Russian for "minority" is "menshinstvo."

Back in 1903, when the Social Democratic Party in Russia was plotting revolution against the Czar, it split into two wings: One, led by Lenin, claimed to be the majority group and took the name "Bolshevik" from "bolshinstvo." It called the other wing "mensheviks" after "menshinstvo."

Both groups helped overthrow the Czarist regime in 1917. But then the Bolsheviks turned on the Mensheviks, threw them in jail, and set up a terroristic dictatorship. The Bolsheviks changed their name to the "Russian Communist Party (Bolshevik)" after they took control, and they have continued to rule under the same name as the only organized political group right up to the present day.

Their headquarters are in Moscow in an 800-year-old fort called the "Kremlin." The head of the party is Joseph Stalin, who not only commands the Communists in Russia but everywhere in the world, including the United States of America.

13. Do you mean the Communists in this country take their orders from Stalin?

Just exactly that, and every one of them knows it sooner or later.

14. Then a "Bolshevik" and a "Communist" are the same thing in meaning, aren't they?

Yes, and they are bad news for everybody else.

15. Well, what did Lenin have in mind when he said give him the child's first eight years?

He meant that, given a child from its infancy, he would turn it into a faceless, obedient, trained Communist slave for life.

16. How?

Here's a quote from an official 1946 guide to teachers of kindergartens in Soviet Russia, which handle children from 3 to 6 years of age:

"The basic habits of Socialist life are formed during this period—order and discipline, friendship and comradeship among children, love of our great motherland, of the Communist Party, of the leaders of the people—."

This kindergarten program is the biggest, broadest, and most elaborate branch of the whole Russian school system.

17. What actually goes on in these kindergartens?

From the same book above quoted:

"Here children play Red Army soldier; in their hands are little flags, on their uniforms and caps are the insignia of infantrymen, tankmen, sailors, and aviators.

"They march in formation to the tune of a martial song."

18. What's the purpose of all this?

Again, that same teachers' handbook tells us the aim is—

"preparation for organized and disciplined labor in higher schools, in production, and in the service of the Red Army."

19. How does that differ from our school system?

We teach children here *how* to think. They teach children *what* to think.

Our kindergartens try to develop children as individuals so each one can have a chance to grow up into the kind of citizen he best can be. Their kindergartens try to stamp each child into a fixed form so that he will serve Communism, and Communism alone, regardless of his own individual ambitions or instincts.

20. Just what makes up the "school system" in America which the Communists want?

There are about 201,100 schools in this country listed by the United States Office of Education. They teach some 31,880,000 students everything from cooking to atomic physics.

Our schools range from public to private to church ownership, and from kindergartens to colleges.

Add to these the thousands of commercial, music, drama, art, business and trade schools not counted in the list above.

Add the research centers, textbook houses, teachers' unions, school supply companies, the National Education Association, and its affiliates.

Each and every one would be wrecked and the pieces taken over.

21. What do you mean by "wrecked"?

Just that. One of the first things that Communists did in Russia when they came to power was to smash the existing school system.

22. How did they do this?

They deliberately broke down college entrance standards and abolished degrees like the B. A., M. A., and Ph. D. Universities became cheap diploma mills.

The lower schools were turned into nothing more than revolutionary clubs, where students were fed godless Communist slogans rather than knowledge. The teachers' authority was destroyed and classrooms became madhouses of disorder with "student councils" deciding courses, discipline, and school policies.

23. Why?

Because the Communists knew they could never control the public mind until they had first smashed the school system as it was.

After the break-down and explosion period, they rebuilt the school system into a tremendous machine for training rather than education.

This was done by installing a new group of teachers loyal to the Communists. These were allowed new and extreme authority over their pupils, who in turn have become cowed, uniformed puppets whose main lesson is to learn to worship Stalin as "teacher, leader, and father."

24. But what about academic freedom?

A teacher under Communism never has freedom, academic or otherwise.

He teaches only what the Government tells him to. And police watch to see that he does so.

25. Would that be so here?

Freedom in every respect would be the first thing to go. Teachers bucking the system would be fired, jailed, or shot.

26. What would they train the pupils here to do after getting the schools under their thumb as they are now in Russia?

To obey, to love, and to hate.

27. To obey whom?

The best answer is from the same teachers' guide, "Pedagogy," earlier quoted:

"Unquestioned obedience and submission to the leader, the teacher or the organizer."

28. To love whom?

From the same source:

"The best people."

29. To hate whom?

Says the Soviet teachers' guide:

"The pupils of the Soviet school must realize that the feeling of Soviet patriotism is saturated with irreconcilable hatred toward the enemies of socialist society."

30. Who are the "best people"?

From that handbook again:

"Our best men and women are banded together in our Communist Party, which directs the entire life of the country."

31. Doesn't that sound like something thought up by Hitler?

Exactly. The Communists were at it before he was and they still are going strong after he has gone. Hitler imitated many tactics of the Communists.

32. Who are these "enemies" the Russian Communists train children to hate?

Anybody and everybody who objects to being dominated all his life long by the Communists. Any loyal citizen of the United States, for instance.

And this training in hate is made twice as deadly by coupling it with formal military training for all children from the fourth grade up.

33. Does any other school system teach hate in the classroom?

Some have, as in Italy, Germany, and Japan. Today, people in those countries are paying the price.

34. And that's what Communism wants to plant over here?

Exactly the same thing.

35. How can we stop it?

Know Communism for what it is. Know Communists for what they are. Find them out, drive them out, and prosecute them by every means possible under the law.

We need more law than is at present on the books in order to do this effectively. See 100 Things You Should Know About Communism in the U. S. A. for more details.

36. What do they want, anyhow?

Power; Communists all have a craze for power.

37. How can I tell a Communist?

Compare his opinions of this or any other country with his opinions of Russia. A Communist will criticize the President of the United States of America, but not Stalin.

38. Who hangs around with the Communists?

Mostly their fellow travelers and front organization dupes, but Communists themselves will go anywhere among any people on orders of their Party leaders.

39. What's a "fellow traveler"?

Someone who follows the Communist Party line without actually carrying a membership card.

40. What's a "front organization"?

Any group that knowingly works for Communist aims or supports Communist propaganda.

41. Are there many around here?

Too many. For details concerning any specific organization, write to the House Committee on Un-American Activities, Room 226, Old House Office Building, or the Department of Justice. Both have published lists of typical Communist fronts, from time to time.

42. Are there many Communist fronts and fellow travelers in the United States school system?

There are, and they are a deadly danger.

43. Who says so?

The Attorney General of the United States, and the United States Office of Education, to mention just two of many official sources.

44. How do they work?

Here is an example given by Dr. Harry Gideonse, president of Brooklyn College:

"A Communist group at an Ohio college recently tried very hard to bring into its ranks a young liberal who was a Phi Beta Kappa and an officer of the Student Council.

"When ideological arguments failed, he was invited to a house off the campus where drinks were served lavishly. He was then told he could bring a girl to the house any time he wanted to, provided he joined the group.

"If he didn't know any girls without bourgeois ideas of morality, he could be introduced to one."

45. That's just the plain old badger game that criminals use everywhere, isn't it?

Surely. The Communists excuse it on the ground that in war anything goes.

46. Did you say "war"?

That's the Communists' own word to describe their attitudes, thoughts, and actions. They themselves say they are "at war" with every person and government in the world that does not submit to Moscow. .

47. What are some of their other "war" tactics on the school campus?

There are many Communists and Communist sympathizers among actors, actresses, authors, musicians, and other artists whose careers are interesting and attractive to young people.

One of the Communist Party's most powerful devices for catching youth is that of using these "big name" agents to spark a campus rally or meeting which has as its real purpose the planting of Party propaganda.

48. Do they meddle in student activities?

Says Dr. Gideonse:

"Perhaps the most effective tactic they employ, however, is their practice of espousing popular causes and protesting militantly against anything which they can make appear as unfair practice, exploitation or discrimination."

49. Do the students know what they're getting into, when they go to these things?

Hardly ever. They go for the fun and excitement, usually, but then the loops and the snares go out and catch all too many.

50. What happens to them, then?

The girl or boy who falls under Communist influence is in danger of losing his whole future as an independent, American citizen.

The same applies for teachers or anybody else.

51. Why?

Because nobody, man, woman or child, can be a Communist and a good citizen of the United States of America at the same time.

52. Again, why?

All Communists everywhere come under the same rule: Absolute obedience in all things to Party orders. Each and every one of these Party orders starts from the Kremlin in Moscow, Russia.

No good American can surrender to that.

53. Do any teachers in our schools actually submit to such a Communist dictatorship?

Here again, read what Dr. Gideonse has to say: ·

"Communist professors and teachers play an important part, of course, in the broad-scale campaign to convert our youth to Stalinism."

54. How do they work?

By slipping propaganda into classroom work and textbooks and by leading gullible students into Red-sponsored campus activities.

55. What's biting these people, anyhow?

Here is at least one part of the answer given by John Hanna, a professor of Columbia University, who was formerly with the Farm Credit Administration and chief analyst with the United States Courts' Administration Office:

"The girls' schools and women's colleges contain some of the most loyal disciples of Russia.

"Teachers there are often frustrated females. They have gone through bitter struggles to attain their positions.

"A political dogma based on hatred expresses their personal attitude."

Politics based on hatred and self-pity has the same appeal for men, too, who feel frustrated by life.

56. Are they open in their hate?

No. Says the same expert:

"They can manipulate admissions and scholarships to obtain radical students. They require courses that give a maximum of indoctrination. They favor students who follow their leadership. At the same time, they are shrewd enough to avoid any open affiliation with Communism."

57. Is this sort of thing confined to the colleges?

Attorney General Tom C. Clark says:

"The Federal Bureau of Investigation has learned that the Communists have started a campaign to recruit our children to their ideology—the younger they are, the better."

58. How about the parents?

Richard Frank, writing in "The Communist," an official Party publication, specifically directed:

"In rural communities, teachers who are among the few educated people are looked up to with tremendous respect. They are in a position to become community leaders.

"As a means of mobilizing the people in the villages and countryside, steps should be taken to try to send Communist teachers into rural communities where they should become active in all community organizations.

"The Party should work actively within Parent-Teachers' Associations and all similar organizations."

59. How about the textbooks?

Dr. Ralph West Robey, Assistant Professor of Banking at Columbia University, made a survey of high school texts a few years ago with one out-and-out Marxist, one "liberal," and one "conservative" scholar to help him.

The results are plain enough for anybody to understand if they *want* to understand.

60. What did the results show?

That the success of the United States of America is played down in too many of our school books and its failures are played up. That the success of Soviet Russia is played up and its failures are played down. This is an important and much-used Communist device.

61. What sort of thing do they say about the United States?

From the report:

"The whole emphasis is placed on the one-third of the population who are underfed, rather than on the two-thirds who are well-fed.

"The textbooks emphasize the small number of large corporations, rather than the large number of small ones. The authors point out the few wealthy people of this country rather than the fact that we have the greatest distribution of wealth in the world."

62. And why shouldn't they do this?

Because the picture of the United States of America given in those texts is false on its face. For all its faults, the United States of America today is the light and hope of the world. Its citizens are the envy of all the rest of mankind. People everywhere want to come here but nobody is leaving here to go to Russia or any other alleged "land of promise."

A true story of the United States would emphasize these facts and show why we have become what we are.

63. Well, why have we?

Because of our basic idea that each person is a free individual who must think and act for himself as an independent human being, and must *not* let himself become a mere cog in a machine. That idea has made us the richest nation the world has ever known.

64. Aren't our natural resources the true source of this wealth?

Certainly not. The same resources were always here, the same soil, timber, minerals, and metals. They never *meant* anything until somebody had the right ideas about how to use them.

65. But don't we have MORE of all the best natural resources than any other people?

No. Russia, for instance, has always had gigantic stores of timber, minerals, farmland, and water power.

The secret of it all is that, never yet, down to this day, has Russia made those things work as we make them work here.

66. Why?

Because the Communists, like the Czars before them, have never really given the people of the country freedom and encouragement to see what they could do with the things lying around before their very eyes.

67. Haven't the Communists expanded industries and agriculture tremendously?

They claim to have done so, but their figures and statistics are so unreliable that the real rate of development is unknown, even to themselves. Only one fact is certain.

68. What?

They have never been able to do enough original planning, development, or expansion on their own, to bring off a real industrial expansion equal to their needs.

Before World War II they had to hire engineers and technicians from the United States, England, and other countries to start their industrial development. Col. Hugh Cooper, the famous American who designed the Soviet system of power dams, is just one of many examples.

Since World War II the Soviets have been copying United States patents, spying in United States factories, and grabbing scientists and engineers from all over Europe to put real brains into their program.

69. What's wrong with their own brains?

The trouble starts with the basic Communist theory that a man should be a cog in a machine, not an independent thinker on his own.

That theory, applied in schools dominated by Communism, turns out people who are trained but *not* educated.

Result: They can't run their country on their own, as we run ours.

70. *Does all that come out in Communist-influenced textbooks?*

It does not. Instead, the authors deliberately falsify facts to support the fiction that the "Communist experiment" has been a "grand and glorious success" in the U. S. S. R.

71. *Do these books teach lies about this country too?*

Yes. For example, some give students the idea that our country is hopelessly ridden with economic evils.

72. *Isn't there something to it?*

There are many ways to answer that, but one ought to be enough. Which nation, in World War II, sent arms and food all over the world to failing Allies and then followed up with armies, navies, and air forces to Europe, Asia, Africa, to outposts in North and South America, and on islands across the seven seas—yet, at home, kept up the highest living standard the world has ever known?

The United States system, as it has been and still is, needs make no apologies to any other.

73. *What's biting these textbook writers, then?*

Communism. Whoever is touched with Communism loses his sense of truth as we know it.

74. *How else have American Communists dug into the United States school system?*

Besides active teaching in public schools, private schools, and church schools, from kindergartens to colleges, they run some schools outright.

75. *You mean there are actually Communist schools in this country?*

Yes.

76. Will you list some?

Here are some typical examples: [3]

School	Location
Jefferson School of Social Science	575 Avenue of the Americas, New York, N. Y.
Jefferson School Annexes:	
Brighton Beach Annex	3200 Coney Island Ave., Brooklyn, N. Y.
Brownsville Annex	108 Watkins St., Brooklyn, N. Y.
Tremont Annex	868 East 180th St., Bronx, N. Y.
Allerton Annex	649 Britton St., Bronx, N. Y.
Philadelphia School of Social Science and Art	1704 Walnut St., Philadelphia, Pa.
People's Educational Center	1717 North Vine St., Hollywood, Calif.
California Labor School	216 Market St., San Francisco, Calif.
Annex	112 West 9th St., Los Angeles, Calif.
Annex	2030 Broadway, Oakland, Calif.
Annex	560 Manlo Dr., Palo Alto, Calif.
Walt Whitman School of Social Science	17 William St., Newark, N. J.
George Washington Carver School	57 West 125th St., New York, N. Y.
Seattle Pacific Northwest Labor School (formerly called Seattle Labor School)	309 Second Ave. North, Seattle, Wash.
Samuel Adams School	37 Province St., Boston 8, Mass.
Abraham Lincoln School	180 West Washington St., Chicago 2, Ill.
Annexes:	
South Side Annex	4448 South Michigan Ave., Chicago, Ill.
Annex	1225 South Independence.
Annex	2409 North Halsted.
School of Jewish Studies	575 Avenue of the Americas, Room 301, New York City.
Ohio School of Social Science and Art	1735 Euclid Ave., Cleveland 15, Ohio.
Tom Paine School	New Rochelle, Westchester, N. Y.
Tom Paine School of Social Science	Academy of Music, Philadelphia, Pa.

[3] At the present time, only the Jefferson School of Social Science, California Labor School, Seattle Pacific Northwest Labor School, and School of Jewish Studies are open. Repeated exposure of their Communist nature has undoubtedly forced the others to suspend operations, but there is little doubt that all will reopen again at the first sign of favorable opportunity, whether under the same name or another. Right now, the work of the People's Educational Center in Los Angeles is being carried on by a branch of the California Labor School of San Francisco.

77. *Some of those schools are named after very famous Americans, aren't they?*

Sure. The Communists started early in the 1930's hiding behind the claim that their program is just the United States Revolution of 1776 brought up to date—a typical Communist propaganda lie.

78. *Who attends these schools?*

Chiefly grown people. Most classes are held at night to attract older people. But there are also children's classes and summer-camp projects for young and old alike.

79. *What do they teach?*

Such courses as history, economics, public speaking, art, drama, and music—all Communist corrupted.

80. *Is any of it on the level at all?*

No. Every course is just so much window dressing for Soviet theory and propaganda.

The whole thing is aimed at luring loyal Americans into becoming Communists.

81. *Are these the only Communist schools?*

No. The Communist Party, U. S. A., also has a network of secret schools, called section, district, and national training schools, in which promising Communists are trained to be leaders in the conspiracy to betray and capture America.

82. *What is the Lenin School?*

The highest college of Communist training. You might say its graduates are all Ph. D.'s of Communism.

83. *Where is it located?*

Moscow, Russia.

84. *What goes on there?*

Carefully selected Communists from the United States and other countries get a free course in factory sabotage, bomb-making, kidnaping, train-wrecking, mutiny, civil warfare, espionage, infiltration, and other methods of wrecking a country.

85. What do you mean "wreck" a country?

The Communist plan for world domination starts with the basic thought that no people will ever submit to Communism without a struggle.

So the top members of the Party in Russia train agents in ways to paralyze a nation from within and capture it, how to destroy its comeback chance, and then how to drive it in Communist harness.

86. How many Americans are Lenin School "graduates"?

An estimated 800 American Communists have been trained there and returned to the United States.

They serve as the high officers of a secret army now being drilled to overthrow our Government.

87. What about Communist Youth groups?

A vitally important instrument of the Communist Party in its plot to get control of America.

88. What is their purpose?

To recruit and train young people for the Communist Party.

89. Can you name some of these?

Here are a few which have been declared subversive by the Attorney General, the Committee on Un-American Activities, or some other official investigating agency:

American Student Union
American Youth Congress
American Youth for a Free World
American Youth for Democracy
California Youth Legislature
Connecticut State Youth Conference
Council of Young Southerners
Friends of the Campus
International Union of Students
Karl Marx Society of Brooklyn College
League of Young Southerners
Los Angeles Youth Committee Against Universal Military Training
Marxist Study Club of City College of New York
Model Youth Legislature of Northern California (1939)
National Student League
National Youth Assembly Against Universal Military Training
Socialist Youth League
Southern Negro Youth Congress
Student Congress Against War
Student Rights Association
Sweethearts of Service Men
Town Meeting of Youth
United Youth Committee Against Lynching
World Federation of Democratic Youth
World Youth Council
Young Communist League
Young People's Records
Young Pioneers of America
Young Progressive Citizens' Committee
Young Workers League

90. *How else do they serve the Communist Party?*

Through strikes—marches—lobbies—rallies—petitions—for the benefit of things the Communists want.

91. *Do they admit Communist control?*

Practically never.

For example, the Young Communist League today goes by the name of American Youth for Democracy, in order to trap loyal young Americans into its ranks.

92. *How important is the AYD?*

Just consider this! It is the American branch of the World Federation for Democratic Youth which is an international Russian-controlled movement to turn the youth of the world to Communism.

93. *What about the Wallace youth groups?*

More tools of the Communist Party.

94. *But the Wallace movement has flopped, hasn't it?*

Figure it out for yourself. Henry Wallace *was* Vice President of the United States from 1941 through 1944, and, therefore, within one heartbeat of the highest office in the land. In 1948 he was candidate for President and polled more than 1,000,000 votes, with the Communist organization using him as its mouthpiece.

Communism gained new recruits through the Wallace campaign, made new contacts, and tapped fresh money. The largest vote ever cast for Communism in this country was registered in 1948 behind Wallace's name.

95. *Are Communists very active in teachers' unions?*

Yes. For instance, the American Federation of Teachers (A. F. L.) in 1941 expelled three of its New York City teachers' unions, with 8,000 members, because the locals were Communist-controlled.

96. *Do many of our teachers play the Communist game?*

The files of our Committee, running back over a ten-year period, show that the Communists have always found the teaching group the easiest touch of all the professional classes for actual Party zealots and fellow travelers.

97. What attracts so many learned men and women to such a murderous and destructive cause?

Sometimes it is frustration. Sometimes it is greed or love of power. Sometimes it is misplaced idealism. But ask them. See if they can give you a good reason for having faith in Communism or any of its works.

98. Are people doing anything about all this?

In some places.

For instance, Ohio State University faculty members are now required to sign the equivalent of non-Communist affidavits. Then, too, in New Jersey, California, Michigan, and Washington State, among others, local authorities have begun investigations of Communist infiltration of schools.

99. Is this sort of thing suppressing academic freedom?

Certainly not. People who demand freedom to teach Communism are demanding the right to teach murder, robbery, revolution, treachery, and disaster. They cannot justify any such demand on any grounds of law, morals, common sense, or reason.

100. What can I do?

FIRST, know the facts.

SECOND, work in your own community to get rid of Communists and Communist influences, whether in the school system or anywhere else.

THIRD, be prepared to face accusations of "witch-hunting," "Red-baiting," "textbook burning," and "strangling academic freedom."

These are all standard smears in the Communist propaganda routine.

ABOVE ALL, remember that whatever you do you must always keep the Constitution of the United States in one hand and common sense in the other. The object here is **NOT** to destroy academic freedom. It is to **STOP COMMUNISM** before it destroys us. The Communists **CAN** be stopped under our system of laws and **MUST** be.

100 THINGS YOU SHOULD KNOW ABOUT

COMMUNISM

AND

LABOR

*The fourth of a series on the Communist conspiracy and its
influence in this country as a whole, on religion, on
education, on labor, and on our government*

* * * *no labor organization can be free under Communism because it is compelled to subordinate the interests of the workers to those of the Communist Party.—*

WILLIAM GREEN, *President, American Federation of Labor*

100 THINGS YOU SHOULD KNOW ABOUT COMMUNISM AND LABOR

> ". . . no labor organization can be free under Communism because it is compelled to subordinate the interests of the workers to those of the Communist Party."—William Green, President, American Federation of Labor.

If you work for a living, there are some facts here you should know. They deal with the future of your job security, working conditions, pay, and union membership, if any.

The aim of Communism is to take control of all these and end forever your chance of living as a free citizen. The aim of this pamphlet, fourth in a series, is to tell you just how Communism works inside the labor movement and what you can do about it.

1. Is this pamphlet an attack on the unions?

No. Read it through and see for yourself.

2. Well, aren't the unions being investigated by your committee?

No. Investigating unions, as such, is **NOT** the committee's job, and so the committee does not do it.

The House Committee on Un-American Activities was started on its way May 20, 1938, with instructions from the United States House of Representatives to expose people and organizations attempting to destroy this country. That is still its job, and to that job it sticks.

3. But haven't I read that its work is just a disguised attack on the unions?

You may have, but that doesn't change the facts which you can check in detail by looking at the printed record of 10 years' hearings now on the shelves of the Library of Congress.

4. What does the record show?

The *first* witness ever to appear before the committee was one of its agents who had joined the German-American Bund to expose Nazi activity in the U. S. A., and the *first* committee witness against Communism was a prominent labor leader.

More than 25,000 pages of testimony have been taken by the committee. These deal with Nazi, Fascist, and Communist activities. When the Nazi movement in the U. S. A. was in its hey-day in 1938, committee investigations were instrumental in sending the ringleaders to jail. Communism was a problem then and remains one now. The committee has continuously exposed its workings—within the secret circles of the Party itself, as well as in the Government, trade-unions, schools, movies, and other fields.

5. Why worry about Communists in the unions, especially?

Because Communists know control of unions will provide a main key to take control of a country.

6. Who was your first witness against Communism?

John P. Frey, president of the Metal Trades Department, American Federation of Labor. His testimony was given August 13, 15, and 16, 1938, and can be found now on pages 91 to 277 of volume I of the committee hearings.

7. What did he say?

He warned American labor that unless it keeps free of Communist encirclement it will one day find itself working for a tyranny that "menaces the structure and form of our Government."

8. Is that all?

No. He filled 186 pages with names, dates, and details to back up a charge that Communism had already begun to dig into American unions.

Frey described Communist penetration of unions in the U. S. A., England, France, and Italy. He warned that over here the central organization of the Congress of Industrial Organizations, National Maritime Union, and United Auto Workers were especially vulnerable and headed for trouble.

9. How did his predictions pan out?

His forecasts proved all too accurate. Communism's grip on the labor movement in France and Italy lasted even through the war and

German occupation and has become, since 1946, a threat to world peace.

In Britain, Communism has been a drain and burden upon even a Socialist government's attempts to hold trade-unionism in line with national policy.

In the U. S. A. the organizations above mentioned have each and every one had a knock-down and drag-out internal fight with Communism. The cost to them and to the Nation was enormous. And let it be remembered they were not the only unions to have terrible internal fights with Communism; and remember, also, the fight is not yet over.

10. *What do the Communists want?*

To dominate your life from the cradle to the grave, in every detail.

11. *Suppose I don't want that?*

They won't ask your approval, if they ever get control.

12. *How do they plan to get control?*

By aggressive war, internal revolution, fraud, trick, corruption of public self-confidence. Any way at all.

13. *If they should get control what would happen to my union?*

It would be wiped out as a union—contract, treasury, constitution, and all. Instead of the union being your agent to bargain a contract for your wages and working conditions, it would become part of the Communist power over you.

14. *Couldn't we just strike, as we do now, for better conditions or higher pay?*

Not a chance.

15. *Why not?*

Because the Government, instead of stepping in to protect your right to strike, would send soldiers around with guns, to kill you.

16. *Kill ME, personally?*

To kill you, personally.

17. *But isn't Communism supposed to help the working man?*

Communism has governed Russia now for more than 30 years, and since 1945 has spread its power over most of Europe and Asia. The record is too plain to fool anybody any longer.

75

Communism, on the evidence of its own works, *grinds down* the workingman. It *does not* lift him up. It *does not* free him. It makes him a *slave of the state.*

18. *Isn't that what they said about the Nazis?*

It is and it was true, too. Both systems are the same for the workingman.

19. *How are they alike?*

Under each the government runs everything, the whole country is taxed to poverty, worked in slavery, and the profits all go to the party in power.

20. *Why can't they be voted out?*

In Nazi Germany there was only one political party in the country—Hitler's. In Communist Russia there is only one political party in the country—Stalin's. The Nazis *were* and the Communists *are* a strictly organized military machine in control of all the weapons and all the power.

21. *Why are some people like that?*

Some people have an overpowering urge to command. Other people sometimes forget to check them until too late. Our problem here and now is to check the Communists.

22. *How, incidentally, can you TELL a Communist?*

Get him in an argument about the United States. He can tell you plenty of things wrong with this country. But ask him to tell you what's wrong with Russia. Even the slickest Communist will sooner or later give himself away on that one. Particularly watch what he says about Stalin.

23. *Is everybody a Communist who criticizes the United States?*

Of course not, but Communists and their dupes make a career of it.

24. *Is everybody a Communist who defends Russia?*

Oh, no. Some of the loudest Russia lovers are only fellow travelers and members of Communist fronts.

25. *What is a fellow traveler?*

Someone who does the Communist Party's work without carrying a Party card.

26. What's a Communist front?

An organization that promotes Communist causes.

27. How can I recognize one?

Basically, by its attitude toward the United States in its dealings with Communists, Communism, and Russia. The more you study the Communist movement the easier it is to spot them, for they all have the habit of using the same language and promoting the same propaganda line.

However, this committee, the Department of Justice, and other official agencies issue from time to time lists of Communist-front organizations and outright Party groups.

Following are typical ones which are now or have been *particularly* trying to influence the ranks of American labor:

*American Committee for European Workers' Relief

American Federation of Labor Trade Union Committee for Unemployment Insurance and Relief

American Labor Party

*American Negro Labor Congress

*American Polish Labor Council

Bronx Victory Labor Committee

*California Labor School

Emergency Trade Union Conference To Aid Spanish Democracy

Farm Research

Greater New York Committee for Employment

*International Labor Defense

*International Workers Order

Joint Committee for Trade Union Rights

King-Connor-Ramsey Defense Committee

*Labor Research Association

National Congress for Unemployment and Social Insurance

*Negro Labor Victory Committee

New York Trade Union Committee To Free Earl Browder

*Revolutionary Workers League

*Seattle Labor School

*Socialist Workers Party

Trade Union Advisory Committee

---

*Asterisks denote organizations cited as Communist dominated by the Attorney General and/or the Committee on Un-American Activities. Organizations not so marked have been cited by the committee only.

Trade Union Committee on Industrial Espionage
Trade Union Committee To Put America Back to Work
*Trade Union Educational League
*Trade Union Unity League
Unemployed Councils and Leagues
Washington (D. C.) C. I. O. Committee to Reinstate Helen Miller
*Workers Alliance
*Workers Party of America
Workers School of New York City
Workmen's Educational Association
Young Workers Leagues

28. Well, getting back to Russia, do they have unions over there at all?

Yes, as Government whips to lay across the workers' backs.

29. Will you tell how?

Better than that, let Victor Kravchenko, an escaped Russian Government official, tell you. Here is his sworn testimony to this Committee:

The local party (Communist) organization, that is through the bureau of the Party, elects one of its suitable members to become president of the trade-union. Generally speaking, the Soviet trade-unions have to see that the workers execute the program.

30. You mean the union helps boss the employees, instead of helping the employees get better wages and working conditions?

Kravchenko answers that the union's job is to see—

that strict discipline is maintained, that there will be NO strikes, that the workers work for wages established by the central government, that the workers carry out all the decisions, resolutions, et cetera, of the party.

31. Doesn't that mean the trade-unions in Russia are really run from the outside by the Communist Party instead of from the inside by the union members?

Kravchenko answers that:

In other words, the Soviet trade-unions function politically, economically, and intellectually like brokers or intermediaries between the Party and people.

*Asterisks denote organizations cited as Communist dominated by the Attorney General and/or the Committee on Un-American Activities. Organizations not so marked have been cited by the committee only.

32. What happens if a Russian wants to quit his job?

Kravchenko again:

Every citizen in the Soviet union has a passport. On the passport is his photograph. There is also a special page on which a stamp is put which indicates the place, date, and type of employment.

If you leave your job in one factory and go to another without the permission of your director you will be prosecuted under the law for violation of the law prohibiting unauthorized change of employment. This refers not only to laborers but to any kind of employee.

For a complete story on working conditions in Communist Russia, read "I Chose Freedom" by Victor Kravchenko. You should find it in any public library.

33. Was it always this way?

No. When the Communists started out in 1917, they kidded the public into thinking that everything would be free and easy. They softened up the unions particularly by making them appear to have a big say in the management of industry.

There have been three big shifts of the gears in Communist control of labor that tell it all.

34. What was the first step?

That was what you might call the honeymoon between the Communists and the people, from 1917 to 1931.

At the very beginning, the Communists promised that regardless of skill or individual ability, everybody would get the same pay, same food, same clothes, and same treatment. A very elaborate paper program of holidays, sick leave, unemployment insurance, and pensions was drawn up.

35. Did it last?

Naturally not. The honeymoon began to come apart in a hurry, but the public didn't get the full bad news in plain language until about 1931, when the second step was taken.

36. What was that?

Stalin in that year announced a "six point program" of industrial policy, as the key to success in the first 5-year plan of expansion.

Any American workingman can understand what Stalin had in mind on learning that he ordered an end to "interference by workers, factory committees, and unions with the operation of plants."

37. *Did he put in a new system?*

That he did. Plant managers were given personal power over their help, but on the other hand they were held personally responsible for success. If they hit the mark set by their own bosses, they got bonuses and promotions. If they missed they got—not fired—**BUT LIQUIDATED.**

Workers were switched to piece rates and put on speed-ups, wherever possible. Instead of all wages being the same, differences in pay for differences in production were glorified.

Stalin called for a 110 percent increase in manufacturing productivity, 75 percent increase in transportation, and 60 percent in construction. He laid on the whip to get it.

38. *How?*

For instance, a man more than 20 minutes late for work could get as much as six months at "corrective labor" in punishment. A penalty was laid on for absenteeism, loafing on the job, or taking too long at meals. The workers had no way out, for their unions were powerless to help them.

39. *Then what happened?*

That's where phase 3 of the workingman's life under Communism came in with the case of Alexei Stakhanov.

40. *What's that?*

Alexei Stakhanov was a coal miner in the Donetz Basin, the region of Russia that compares with our own western Pennsylvania or West Virginia. The Communists dug him up in 1933 or 1934 and made him a propaganda hero. All he did, if anything, was to hit on some ideas of dividing up work and making each motion count for more production than before.

41. *Isn't that just the old speed-up trick?*

American industry has been working for many years to show how a shovel, a pick, or a machine can be handled to get more out of it than before and to make labor less burdensome.

The difference between that and the way the Communists used Stakhanov is something that should interest any American union member.

42. *What was that?*

Well, in 1935, a "Congress of Stakhanovites" was called in Moscow with Stalin presiding. These "Stakhanovites" were a hand-picked group of Communist Party agents from all industries and all sections of the country chosen specifically to set a production pace far above the average man's ability. They were given a big time in Moscow, told the country's fate depended on them, and then sent back home to spread the "gospel"—that hard work would thereafter be harder than ever.

Stakhanovites began to go up the ladder both in the Communist Party and in actual factory management. Eventually the most severe Stakhanov speed-up policies became factory standards, that punished anybody falling behind. *But wages did not keep up with production.*

43. *What did the unions do then?*

Just what the management told them—To produce or else.

44. *Who was the management?*

The Communist Party, which runs everything in Russia. It runs the Government, the factories, the schools, the hospitals, the churches, the homes, the work and the play of the people, from cradle to grave.

In Russia, the Communist Party has a monopoly on decisions. It does the thinking and everybody else does the working. The Communists make policy. The people take the consequences. The Communists enjoy the profits and the public pays the bill.

45. *That is some change, isn't it, from the old honeymoon the workers started on back in 1917–18 when Communism had just come to power?*

You said it.

46. *What made the change?*

Ask the Communists. The fact remains that not for the past 20 years have unions in Russia had any influence on management, nor any power to make collective bargains for workers, change any working conditions, or fix their wages.

In addition, the Russian government has thrown 14,000,000 to 20,000,000 men and women into slave labor camps, where they are forced to work inhumanly long hours at hard tasks under barbarous conditions. These slaves are mostly politicians, farmers, priests, et cetera, whose only "crime" was disagreement with the Communists.

47. *And that's what Communism would do for us over here, if it could?*

That's what it did in Russia, even before World War II, and has done since in countries it has captured in Europe and Asia. It would do the same here.

48. How can Communism be stopped, here?

First, detect the Communists at work around you. Second, expose them and all their connections. Third, wherever possible, force their prosecution under the laws of our country.

49. What do Communists go after in an American union?

Key jobs, such as president, business agent, secretary, treasurer, or counsel at law. They almost never stay down in the rank and file except on orders to hide out there for the particular purpose of sniping at the union officers if these are all anti-Communist.

50. Why don't they all try for union president?

The president of a union is usually too public a figure for effective work as a Communist. The real power, day by day, lies in monopolizing the jobs *around* the president.

51. Do Communists join unions to improve the conditions of the workingman?

They join specifically to make all unions, in the words of Stalin, "schools of Communism." That covers everything.

52. Suppose there is a conflict between the union's interest and the Communist Party's orders?

The Communist Party comes first in every Communist's life. You have to bear in mind that when anybody joins the Communist Party he becomes literally a soldier in a "class war," as the Communists call it.

53. What do you mean by "war"?

The Communists consider themselves actually at war with every person and every government in the world that does not take orders from Moscow. They, themselves, live under a "class war" discipline more strict than our Army, Navy, or Marines do.

54. How could they help their class war by wrecking a union?

Take the case of a general strike. Communists try to organize these on the slightest excuse, regardless of the effect on the union movement as a whole, on the survival of unions crushed by the consequences, and regardless of the wholesale suffering and hardship brought down upon working families in the process. Their theory is that the more misery they can cause in the present the easier it will be for them to grab control in the future.

55. What role is played in the union movement by Communist lawyers?

They often serve as the direct channel between the Communist Party and the union. Although not elected by the membership and not responsible to it, they often exercise monopoly control of collective bargaining and union policy.

They are responsible for all kinds of legal tricks to perpetuate the control of Communist officials and stifle all opposition.

56. What union role is played by a Communist accountant or treasurer?

He knows the most intimate details of union money and is in a position to report the most confidential information to the Communist Party. Also he can cover up Communist use of union money.

57. How can the union treasury be used for Communist purposes?

Through contributions to Communist organizations or individuals, who siphon off funds to Communist use either directly or through Communist-dominated printing plants, meeting halls, newspapers (for advertising), front organizations, or to "entertainers" supporting Communist campaigns for "justice" to somebody or other.

58. How does a Communist educational director operate in a union?

He conducts Communist propaganda courses and invites Communist speakers to address union members. He presents Communist films and entertainment. He recruits members for the Communist Party. He trains selected personnel for intelligence and sabotage service. He popularizes Communist literature in the union library.

59. How does a Communist editor slant a union paper?

By printing articles from Communist writers. By giving a Communist twist to editorials and news items. By advertising and supporting Communist activities and organizations. By reviewing Communist books. By employing Communist cartoonists. You can tell by the way he compares U. S. and Russian affairs.

60. What post do the Communists try to capture in a shop?

Shop steward. This is important because it gives the Communist an opportunity to manufacture grievances, to incite strikes, distribute Communist literature, and collect funds for Communist purposes and engage in spying. Actually he is aiming to make "every factory a fortress" for Communism, as advised by Lenin.

61. Do the Communists rig union elections?

Plenty. Just before the election they railroad through a nominations committee stacked with Communists and sympathizers, and put over an "approved" slate of nominees with but one choice for each office printed on the ballot.

Opposition candidates are often framed on false charges of violating union rules, nonpayment of dues, etc. Ballots are premarked and forged. A committee of Communist stooges counts the ballots in secret.

62. How can they do these things, if they are in the minority?

It's easy, if you let them. They come to meetings carefully organized. They throw in at the beginning a long list of objections and proposals to change the regular order of business, whatever it may be.

They keep it up until the opposition wears out, scatters, gets tired, and goes home. Then they slam through their real plans and the next day the majority wakes up to find itself committed to something it never had in mind.

63. Can you tell me what a "Communist diamond" is?

One of their operating formations. They look at a union hall as a battlefield. One Communist unit takes the front row, center. One sits half way back on the right side. One, half way back on the left side. The fourth unit takes the back row, center.

They actually form a four-point diamond that way, covering the hall.

64. What then?

The four units work on signals just like a baseball team. They hiss, boo, make motions, shout down opposition, start fights, yell "Fire," or do whatever their boss on the scene directs. You would be surprised how much trouble a small number of disciplined rioters can make that way, unless you've seen it work.

65. Can anybody do anything about it?

Sure. Put your own diamond in their places, take the play away from them, wear the Communists down instead of letting them wear *you* down.

66. How do they get into a union in the first place?

Here is a description by David Dubinsky, a very successful union leader who has had to slap the Communists down, first-hand:

The Communist technique is simple. The Party agent forms acquaintance of a member of a union which is marked for capture. They form a "cell" or

84

"fraction" of a few like-minded members. With the help of the Party agent a program is prepared. Naturally, it follows the Communist Party line.

67. What then?

Says Dubinsky:

The innocent is introduced to an important party functionary or well-known party speaker; he is taken to cocktail parties and dances and no time is lost in introducing him to attractive partners. The next scene is at the union meeting.

At the meeting, the Communist faction takes over and wears down the majority, as described in the answers to the questions just above.

68. Well, don't they do some good just the same?

Let Dubinsky, the labor leader, answer that:

The Communists refer to themselves as the "vanguard of labor." Nothing could be further from the truth. They have disrupted many unions with their factional quarrels and have left in their wake many saddened and disillusioned members, destroyed businesses, and blasted hopes. Far from being "progressives" as they claim, they are really "dynamic reactionaries" as someone has called them.

69. Can you give an example of a union ruined by Communism?

Let Dubinsky tell it, again:

Although our union is free of the Communist menace today it was not always so. In 1926 the Communist Party, through its demagogic propaganda and exaggerated promises, was able to attract many of our members. It thus managed to obtain control of our New York organization and succeeded in plunging the coat and suit industry into a general strike.

It took 10 years for us to recover from the criminal and stupid Communist-led strike of 1926 which cost $4,500,000 and left in its wake a chaotic industry and a crippled union.

70. Is it possible to throw the Communists out of control, once they have wormed into a union?

It is no easy job. The founder of Communist government in Russia was Nikolai Lenin and his word to this day is sacred to Communists. He laid down the rule to:

agree to any sacrifices and even if need be to resort to all sorts of stratagems, artifices, illegal methods, to evasions and subterfuges, only so as to get into the trade-unions, to remain in them and to carry on Communist work within them at all costs.

But they **CAN** be defeated if you work hard enough.

71. Could a union refuse membership or office to a Communist?

All it has to do is to make Communist Party membership contrary to the union constitution and enforce that clause. The law of the

United States can be used to help do that. If your union lawyer doesn't have the information on that, tell him to get it from the Government.

72. What unions have the Communists controlled?

In 1944, the Committee on Un-American Activities found the following unions to have "Communist leadership . . . strongly entrenched":

American Communications Association (CIO)

International Federation of Architects, Engineers, Chemists, and
  Technicians (CIO)

International Fur and Leather Workers Union (CIO)

International Longshoremen's and Warehousemen's Union (CIO)

International Union of Fishermen and Allied Workers of America
  (CIO)

International Union of Mine, Mill, and Smelter Workers (CIO)

International Woodworkers of America (CIO)

Marine Cooks and Stewards Association of the Pacific Coast (CIO)

National Maritime Union of America (CIO)

State, County, and Municipal Workers
  of America (CIO) ⎫
  ⎬ Merged to form United
United Federal Workers of America ⎰ Public Workers of America
  (CIO)

Transport Workers Union of America (CIO)

United Cannery, Agricultural, Packing, and Allied Workers of America (CIO)

United Electrical, Radio, and Machine Workers of America (CIO)

United Farm Equipment and Metal Workers of America (CIO)

United Furniture Workers of America (CIO)

United Gas, Coke, and Chemical Workers of America (CIO)

United Office and Professional Workers of America (CIO)

United Packinghouse Workers of America (CIO)

United Shoe Workers of America (CIO)

United Stone and Allied Products Workers of America (CIO)

73. Are all these unions still under Communist leadership?

Some have belatedly tried to clean out the Communists—notably the Transport Workers Union under the aggressive direction of its president, Michael Quill. But in a number of these, such as the powerful United Electrical Workers', and Longshoremen's Unions, Communists are still in the saddle.

74. What would the Communists do in the event of war between the United States and the Soviet Union?

They say themselves that they would "stop the manufacture and transport of munitions," as well as "the transport of all other materials essential to the conduct of war through mass demonstrations, picketing, and strikes." They would try to "stall the (American) war machine in its tracks."

75. Have the Communists ever carried out such a policy in the United States?

Yes, during the Stalin-Hitler pact (1939–41) they caused terrible strikes that delayed U. S. rearmament. For example, Allis-Chalmers, Milwaukee; International Harvester, Harvill plant in Los Angeles; Vultee Aircraft, North American Aviation, Los Angeles; Aluminum Co. of America, Cleveland; the Mine, Mill and Smelter Workers at Trona, Calif., and in Connecticut brass factories, all were led out by the Communists.

76. What could the above cited American Communications Association do in case of war?

This outfit is in our cable offices and in the radio control rooms of our merchant ships and commercial airfields. They could garble messages so as to sink ships, wreck planes, tap intelligence channels, and isolate us from the rest of the world.

77. Would the International Longshoremen's and Warehousemen's Union give us anything to worry about?

This has 75,000 members. They have effective control of many ports in the U. S. A. and more than once have used it to paralyze shipping. Communist domination of this union in wartime could wreck the whole U. S. fighting power.

78. What could the Transport Workers Union do?

Paralyze bus, subway and trolley transportation in some of our largest cities. Without transportation, life in these cities would come to a standstill.

This union, which claims 100,000 members, could also tie up some of our most important air lines.

79. How about the United Electrical, Radio, and Machine Workers of America?

The leading electrical and machine plants, manufacturing important parts for guns, tanks, torpedoes, range finders, sound detectors, altimeters, gyroscopes, aerial cameras, motors, and other vital equipment, are at its mercy.

The union, which claims 600,000 members, is banned from representing our Nation's atomic workers.

80. Surely the United Public Workers of America would not be a menace, would it?

There are 15,000 members of this union in the Panama Canal Zone, alone. Many of the other 71,000 members are stationed at navy yards, arsenals, experimental stations, the State Department, and throughout our Government agencies.

81. Well, how do you know Communism has any power in any of these listed unions?

Because of the men who hold positions of critical influence in them.

Here are some examples of Communist officers:

Name	Union	Office*
Harry Bridges	International Longshoremen's and Warehousemen's Union, CIO.	President.
Samuel Burt	International Fur and Leather Workers' Union, CIO.	Vice president; also manager, Joint Board of Fur Dressers and Dyers.
Philip M. Connelly	Los Angeles CIO Council	Secretary.
Julius Emspak	United Electrical, Radio and Machine Workers of America, CIO.	Secretary-treasurer.
Abram Flaxer	United Public Workers of America, CIO.	President.
Julius Fleiss	International Fur and Leather Workers' Union, CIO.	Business agent, Furriers Joint Council.
Ben Gold	International Fur and Leather Workers' Union, CIO.	President.
Donald Henderson	Food, Tobacco, Agricultural and Allied Workers' Union of America, CIO.	Do.
James Lustig	United Electrical, Radio and Machine Workers of America, CIO.	Representative, District 4.
James Matles	United Electrical, Radio and Machine Workers of America, CIO.	National organizational director.
Irving Potash	International Fur and Leather Workers' Union, CIO.	Vice president; also manager, Furriers Joint Council of New York.
William Sentner	United Electrical, Radio and Machine Workers of America, CIO.	President, District 8.
Maurice Travis	International Union of Mine, Mill and Smelter Workers, CIO.	Secretary-treasurer.

*Offices listed above were held by the men in question as recently as the year 1948. If there have been any changes, they have not come to the committee's notice.

88

82. How else?

Because these unions not only endorse Communist aims in union matters but also in matters of United States national policy.

83. Can you give some examples?

During the Stalin-Hitler Pact, Joseph Selley, president of the American Communications Association, CIO, led a movement against U. S. armaments, saying "Don't give us any baloney about 'patriotism' and 'national defense'."

Harry Bridges in 1934 won the high praise of the Communist International for involving the International Longshoremen's and Warehousemen's Union in a general strike.

The Transport Workers Union has just won a violent internal struggle for power led by President Michael Quill against John Santo, former International Organization Director, who is subject to deportation proceedings for being a member of an organization "advocating and teaching the overthrow by force and violence of the government of the United States."

We could multiply this many times.

84. Do you hold the rank and file of these unions responsible for the actions of a few individuals?

The rank and file allow such men to command them.

Of course, we do not indict all the members of any union as Communistic just on that account, but we do call their attention to the things that are being done in their name.

The responsibility for cleaning up their unions rests primarily upon them and with courageous, patriotic action they can always throw the Communists out.

85. Just the same, isn't Communism a working-class movement?

Absolutely not. It is a *revolutionary* movement.

A working-class movement seeks to better the state of labor. This revolutionary movement seeks to destroy things as they are, with the aim to seize power and put it in the hands of one political party— the Communist Party.

86. But don't Communists promise that when they get power they will hand it over to the workers?

Yes, they promise that. Now point to one place in the world where they have lived up to that promise. There is none, of course.

89

The standard of living in Russia under Communism is barely above that of India and China. The people live in abject poverty, while the bigwigs among the Communists live better than most millionaires do in this country.

87. Can you give some figures?

For example, as of 1947, a Russian had to work 22 days for money enough to buy a suit of clothes. An American could get a much better suit for 20½ hours' work.

Even today in Russia, a man works for 32 hours to buy a cotton dress for his wife. In America a man works only 4 hours to buy his wife a better dress.

In Russia it takes a worker 108 hours to earn a pair of shoes. In America he can do it in 9 hours.

In Russia a man must work one hour and forty minutes to buy a bottle of beer. In America he needs to work only six minutes.

The same comparison works out all along the line for food, shelter, and other necessities of life.

88. Where do Communists come from in America?

Contrary to what you may have heard, the record shows that relatively few Communists spring directly from the people who work at hard labor. Mainly, Communists come from the so-called "middle class"—doctors, lawyers, teachers, actors, writers, accountants, other white-collar workers, and even at times among the clergy.

Most Communists have never worked with their hands, except where and when directed by the Party. This is the case not only in the United States but all over the world.

89. What is the World Federation of Trade Unions?

The WFTU was formed by a group of labor leaders in September 1945, as an effort intended to carry over into peace the wartime alliance of the United States, Great Britain, Russia, and other countries, insofar as the labor organizations of those countries were involved. But it has not succeeded because of Communist infiltration.

90. Does labor in this country support it?

The American Federation of Labor has refused to affiliate. On September 17, 1948, President William Green, of the A. F. of L., said:

Opposing our efforts to bring security, prosperity, and peace to the workers of Europe is ranged a powerful fifth column of Moscow, which masquerades under the name of the World Federation of Trade Unions.

91. How about the CIO?

The CIO pays international dues to the WFTU. At the recent CIO convention a resolution was adopted aiming to bring the WFTU back to the purpose for which it was founded.

92. What labor organizations abroad back the WFTU?

The labor federations in the Soviet-controlled countries of Poland, Albania, Bulgaria, Hungary, Rumania, Czechoslovakia, and Yugoslavia.

In Italy, the Confederation of Labor, headed by Di Vittorio, a Communist.

In France, the Confederation of Labor which is almost entirely Communist-dominated.

In the Western Hemisphere, the Latin-American Federation of Labor, headed by Vicente Lombardo Toledano, which consistently attacks the United States and its foreign policies.

93. Are they catching on to it abroad?

Arthur Deakin, one of the leaders of the labor movement in Britain, and a former president of the WFTU, itself, warned the British Trade Union Congress this year:

The Communists have captured the World Federation of Trade Unions and are using it as a medium for advancing Soviet propaganda, not only in Europe, but throughout the world.

94. What is the American Communists' attitude toward the WFTU?

William Z. Foster, head of the Communist Party in this country, has stated that:

It is imperative that the world's workers, through the World Federation of Trade Unions, should intervene in the proceedings of the United Nations.

95. Have the Communists actually used the international labor movement in recent years to capture governments?

Specifically, in Poland, Czechoslovakia, and each of the other European governments now Communist dominated.

96. What's a good program for an American union man against Communism?

Here is one given by James B. Carey, secretary-treasurer of the CIO:

Full exposure of the Communists, plus a strong progressive policy "far in advance of the bogus progressivism of the Communists."

Swift, flexible infighting that defeats the Communists at their own game within the union.

97. What is the CIO doing about this itself?

At its latest convention, CIO President Philip Murray officially denounced "unfit" unions and the CIO executive board was given broad power to organize workers in fields where such unions had "failed."

Also, there has been an extensive house cleaning of State and city industrial union councils, which, according to Carey, were "often converted into virtual soapboxes of Communist propaganda."

98. Which unions did Murray call "unfit"?

The United Office and Professional Workers of America (CIO) and the United Public Workers of America (CIO), which will be dealt with extensively in the next pamphlet of this series, "100 Things You Should Know About Communism and Government."

99. What is the biggest single blow the Communists have felt from the CIO?

Expulsion of the Greater New York CIO Council—key unit in the whole Communist program. This took place November 20, 1948.

100. Well, then, can't we just relax now and forget it?

At your peril. We promised this pamphlet, as a whole, will answer question 1. Read it again and see why we say what we do in the answer to question 100.

100 THINGS YOU SHOULD KNOW ABOUT

COMMUNISM

AND

GOVERNMENT

*The fifth of a series on the Communist conspiracy and its
influence in this country as a whole, on religion, on
education, on labor, and on our government*

"The American Soviet government will be organized along the broad lines of the Russian Soviets. * * * The American Soviet government will join with the other Soviet governments in a world Soviet Union."

——WILLIAM Z. FOSTER
Chairman, Communist Party, U. S. A.

100 Things You Should Know About Communism and Government

Our Government is under attack. The enemy is Communism. If Communism were to win, there would be no United States Constitution, Courts, President, or Congress.

The American Republic would be wiped out, and in its place there would be a system with which freedom cannot live.

Here, in this fifth and final one of a series of pamphlets, are the facts on what Communism has already done to, and aims to do to, the Government of the United States.

1. Are Communists traitors?

This whole pamphlet is to help you make up your own mind on that. The facts speak louder than words.

2. Are Communists loyal?

To Stalin. Not to the U. S. A.

3. Are Communists spies?

Anytime they are ordered to be by their Party.

4. Would Communists support our Government in war with Russia?

The sworn testimony of their present leader in this country is "no."

5. Do American Communists EVER uphold our Government?

When it suits Moscow's purposes. For instance, from 1939 to 1941, while Germany and Russia were on the same side in the European war, American Communists sabotaged our arms factories, and spied on our Government for Hitler as well as for Stalin. They even tried to stir sedition and rebellion in the armed forces. But when Germany attacked Russia, they wrapped themselves with the U. S. flag overnight and immediately demanded that we go to war—for Russia's sake.

6. *Are there any Communists in our Government now?*

We hate to say it, but nobody knows whether there are 3 or 3,000, even though $17,000,000 have been spent by the President in the last two years to find out. Read on for details.

7. *Well, what do they want?*

To capture our Government any way they can, in order to use it against us.

8. *Why do Communists want to upset things as they are?*

Communists believe in Communism. Nothing else. They mean to enslave the world under Communist command.

9. *Do they admit that?*

V. I. Lenin, founder of Communist government in Russia in 1917, at that time declared "the historical mission of the Soviets to be the gravediggers, the heir and the successor" to the governments of the world.

10. *And they're still headed that way?*

Look at the roll call of conquered nations across Europe and Asia. See how Communist rule has grown in thirty-one years, until now it commands more people than any other system of government on earth, more than any ever has before in the history of the world.

11. *What's the secret of its success?*

The carelessness and indifference of other people.

12. *How do you mean?*

Communism is a terrible international organization of spies, wreckers of civilization, and destroyers of nations.

It is directed and managed as a world army from the city of Moscow, Russia.

Communists in every country are strictly disciplined, closely organized Russian agents.

But they overturn governments and destroy nations **NOT** through their own power. They do it through the theft of others' power.

96

13. How do they get at this power?

By filtering into key spots of control while the majority in any country still thinks Communism is "just a crackpot idea" and "Communists are just another political pressure group."

14. Where are these keys to power?

In the government, in the schools, the churches, and labor unions. See the first four pamphlets of this series:

> 100 Things You Should Know About Communism in the U. S. A.
> 100 Things You Should Know About Communism and Religion.
> 100 Things You Should Know About Communism and Education.
> 100 Things You Should Know About Communism and Labor.

15. Are Communists in this country part of this world movement?

Not "movement." The right word is "conspiracy." All Communists, everywhere, are a part of it. A Communist in China, in Washington, D. C., in London, Paris, Berlin, or Rome, is the same as any other Communist.

Every one is an agent of Moscow working for the capture of the world.

16. Well, supposing they win here, what happens?

The Constitution will go. The free American Republic will be dead.

17. Would we have a President as we have today?

No.

18. Would we have a Supreme Court?

No.

19. Would we have a Congress?

No.

20. How about the State, county, and city Governments?

Gone.

21. Well, how would the Government be run?

By one man, the top U. S. Communist. He would be our President, Congress, Supreme Court, and everything else, all rolled into one. And even HE would only be an office boy for a man in Moscow— Stalin.

22. Would we even be known as the United States of America any longer?

No. William Z. Foster, present head of the Communist Party, U. S. A., says we would be known as "Soviet America" if the Communists take over. Our symbol of freedom, the Stars and Stripes, would be replaced by the Red flag of Russia.

23. And that's what Communism wants to deliver here?

Right.

24. Suppose we didn't like it?

Too late. Once in power, the Communists kill and destroy until there is not even a seed-bed left for opposition to their monopoly of power.

25. How does the Communist Party keep such a tight control of power where it is in command?

The Communists own the guns.

26. But don't they promise to help people live better if they get into power?

That they do. But name one place where they have delivered.

27. What do the Communists themselves get out of it?

Rich livings where they are on top, but the main thing is that Communists all have a lust for power which drives them night and day. Government by their system is the only thing that satisfies their lust.

28. And you say some Communists have sneaked into our Government, as it is today?

Yes. And we repeat, nobody knows how many.

29. When and how did they break in?

You'll have to review a little U. S. and world history to get a clear picture. There have been changes in direction for the Communists over here from time to time, each of which has had its influence on Communists in government.

30. What was the first development?

The Communist Party in the United States was organized at Chicago, Illinois, September 1–7, 1919. For ten years thereafter, it went through a series of violent internal shake-ups and factional fights that kept it from concentrating very effectively on our own governmental machinery.

Furthermore, the official Party theory then was that we were on the verge of a crack-up, anyhow, and would be taken over any day. Therefore filtering into our governmental machinery was regarded as a waste of time.

31. Did they really say that we were cracking up?

Here's a quote from Stalin, May 6, 1929:

I think the moment is not very far off when a revolutionary crisis will develop in America.

He said that in the course of a speech outlining a complete reorganization of the Communist set-up over here to prepare for what he called "its historic task" of taking over the U. S. A. in crisis.

32. Well, didn't we actually HAVE a "revolutionary crisis," just as he predicted?

No, even though the U. S. A. and the rest of the world all plunged together into a terrible economic slump.

33. How did Russia do in that slump?

Curiously enough, the government most violently shaken of all in the world was Stalin's. The Communist Party in Russia broke in two and Stalin had to spend the better part of the next eight years shooting and killing off his opposition.

As for the people of Russia, they suffered the most terrible privations. Millions literally starved to death. The standard of living dragged along barely above that of China and India.

34. How about the U. S. A.?

We had ample power under our Constitution to act, and so did. The United States and its citizens found a peaceful road out of the depression without any Moscow-type purges, killings, or violence.

In fact, we not only recovered from the depression under our tried and true Constitutional system, but even financed and fought the most terrible war in history, and Soviet Russia itself would have been destroyed without our aid.

Today, still under that system, we are the hope and envy of the world. Russia is not.

35. What's all that got to do with Communists in our Government?

It's just to remind you of some serious facts of life and to point out by comparison the different effects of freedom and slavery.

Our system still survives IN SPITE of Communists within and without. On the other hand, the Communists, even with a total monopoly of power, still have to use guns to rule.

36. Well, when did they begin to invade OUR Government?

The fatal official turning point was November 16, 1933, the day when the Government of the United States granted diplomatic recognition to the Soviet government of Russia. That ended the futile first phase of Communist activity in this country and a second far more deadly development got under way.

37. What was that?

The famous "Trojan Horse" or "United Front" program by which Communists were directed to say less in public about violent revolution and DO more toward corrupting from within.

38. By the way, what did our Government get, officially, in return for granting Stalin diplomatic recognition?

Promises to (a) settle all outstanding debts between the two countries, (b) develop mutual trade, (c) end Communist propaganda against our Constitution, and (d) refuse support to the Communists here seeking to destroy our country.

.39. Were any of these promises kept?

Not one.

40. Well, what actually happened?

In Russia itself, the crisis of the Communist Party continued its bloody way. More than 1,000,000 Party members (about a third of the total membership) were expelled in 1933, alone.

The next year an open reign of terror and assassination swept the country. The terrible "purge trials" began and it was obvious to the world that Communism was at the point of real collapse.

But it was saved by U. S. recognition and by that afore-mentioned "United Front" and "Trojan Horse" program.

41. What form did this strategy take over here in the U. S. A.?

Communists stopped operating apart from everybody else and instead began to join other people's movements and to offer their own disciplined forces to promotors of special causes and public issues with intent to capture "fellow travelers" and "Communist front" organizations.

42. What is a "fellow traveler"?

Anybody who allies himself with Communists in anything is a fellow traveler. He is a deadly weapon, for he deceives others and often himself, that Communism can be led to peaceful ways.

43. Is that possible?

Neither in fact nor in theory. The Communists have always made it basic in their thoughts that **VIOLENCE** is inevitable in their struggle for the world. And in all their captures, from Russia in 1917 down to China in 1948, they have **USED** violence as their weapon.

44. What's a "Communist front"?

Any organization that lends itself to Communist purposes. This committee has just issued a pamphlet, 144 pages long, on this subject listing examples. It is entitled "CITATIONS by Official Government Agencies of Organizations and Publications Found to be Communist or Communist Fronts." You can get it by writing the committee, or the Government Printing Office.

45. When did these spring up in the U. S. A.?

Immediately upon U. S. recognition of Soviet Russia. Communists, fellow travelers, and front agents promptly flooded Washington, and began to worm their way into the Government of the United States.

46. Where did they show up, mostly?

The main inflow was through the Public Works Agency, Works Progress Administration, Agricultural Adjustment Administration, and National Recovery Administration, during the years 1933–36.

The Federal Art Project, Federal Writers' Project, Federal Theatre Project, and such organizations introduced them in large numbers.

47. Did they stay in these?

By no means. Within a few years, Communist lawyers, accountants, executives, and scientists were solidly entrenched in Washington in various Government departments.

48. Who let them do it?

You. The voting public is the real power of Government in this country. Public indifference to the realities of Communism in past years caused indifference on the part of governmental officials.

49. How do you mean "indifference"?

Here is an example given by J. Edgar Hoover:

The FBI submitted a 57-page report to the Federal Security Agency on March 7, 1942, on Doxey Wilkerson. The investigation recorded interviews with persons who stated that he was a member of the Communist Party. Following submission of the report, we were advised by the Federal Security Agency that further investigation failed to show Wilkerson was "subversive or disloyal to our Government."

50. Well, was he?

The Hoover report answers that:

Wilkerson subsequently transferred to OPA and resigned on June 19, 1943. Within 24 hours he announced his new job as a "Communist Party organizer." He was subsequently appointed a member of the National Committee of the Communist Party. To be eligible for service with the National Committee, one "must have been a member of the Party in continuous good standing for at least four years."

51. You blame me for that sort of thing?

Yes. Until the general public demands it, offices of the Government will always tend to be slack about cracking down.

52. How did the Communists use the federal theatre, writers, and other such projects?

To present Communist propaganda plays, to feature Communist actors, to distribute Communist propaganda in Government books, pamphlets, and art work.

53. Can you give a sample of Communism in the WPA theatre project?

Here is the testimony of a confidential investigator for the head of the WPA, regarding two of the Federal Theatre Project Plays:

* * * there was one with the title *"Triple A Plowed Under."* That was one play which on the opening night required 30 New York policemen to guard the play and prevent a riot.

It contained a scene in which the secretary of the Communist Party condemns the judiciary of the United States Government. Such characters as George Washington and Andrew Jackson were removed from the play in order to give a prominent part to the secretary of the Communist Party, Earl Browder.

The conclusion of the play is the establishment of a political party in accordance with the wish expressed by the secretary of the Communist Party, expressed by Mr. Earl Browder himself in a radio broadcast a short time previous to the production. * * *

Then there was *"The Class of '29."* The script called for the cast to carry the Red Soviet banner. While they start in the beginning of a show, they do not really carry the props used for the production. So they carried something which was to take the place of the Soviet banner.

54. How about writing?

Well, for example, Committee Report issued January 3, 1939, pp. 31 and 32, tells in detail how Communists slipped their propaganda into the WPA writers program of "state guides", a series of supposedly historical and descriptive studies of the 48 states.

55. How about the art project?

Same story. In numerous communities, after post offices and other federal buildings had been decorated at considerable expense to the taxpayers, paintings were covered over or removed upon public demand. Communist-corrupted art work, however, can still be found in many public places to this day.

56. What was the idea of all this?

The Communists try to tilt public sentiment their way by propaganda in art, literature, and music. The chance to carry on such a campaign at the taxpayers' expense was a stroke of fortune they naturally would not overlook. But it was only a sideline to their main job.

57. What was that?

The same it remains today.   Espionage.

58. How did they set up this spy system?

Naturally, it is impossible for any outsider to know the full story, but the main outlines are clear.

Sometime in the 1930's the Party planted secret operatives high in the U. S. executive branch and began to place around them a corps of skilled agents.

59. Have any of them been identified?

Some extremely important officials have been accused by witnesses before this committee as either Communists or fellow travelers.   Details further along in this pamphlet.

60. Has your committee ever conducted a real investigation into the departments to clean up these matters?

Not on the scale we would like.   Such facts as we have learned are just byproducts in carrying out the committee's mission from the House to investigate subversive activity of all kinds, wherever found, report on the facts to the House and recommend legislation accordingly.

61. Getting down to details of what you HAVE found, how about Communism in federal employee unions?

The United Public Workers of America (CIO) is deep into federal service and it is Communist-controlled.

The UPWA has 15,000 members in the highly strategic Panama Canal Zone and the U. S. District Attorney there has openly declared this situation a public danger.

62. How about the Army, Navy, etc.?

Communists are in there, too.   How many we don't know.

63. How about atomic energy?

The best indication is the fact that the Atomic Energy Commission this fall of 1948 had to withdraw recognition of certain unions because the union's officers would not sign non-Communist affidavits.

The AEC has now ruled that for "security reasons" the officers of *ALL* unions with which it deals must be put through a federal loyalty investigation whether the employees are working for the Government or for some contractor with AEC.

64. Is this going to be the rule for ALL federal agencies, now?

We recommend it, not only for all federal but state and other governmental agencies.

The disclosure of Communist union officers is not only important to safe government but also to the protection of unions themselves from Communist sabotage.

65. Do Communists ever try to fix elections?

As in every other field, they lay a poisonous hand on the ballot box. They sometimes run candidates in the open under the Communist label. More often they enter into corrupt bargains to back their stooges under cover.

66. Any proof?

For example, in the 1940 Presidential election year, this committee made a special inquiry into Communist voting tactics.

Surveys in Maryland, West Virginia, Pennsylvania, Kentucky, and Ohio all unearthed wholesale frauds.

More than 100 indictments were brought on the basis of evidence the committee disclosed and between 50 and 60 convictions followed. But that did not end the problem. Communists still try to corrupt the ballot box at every opportunity.

67. What is their method?

Communist candidates circulate petitions for nominations and obtain signatures, without disclosing WHAT party the candidates represents.

They also have been convicted of forging signatures, using false names and generally showing contempt for the law.

68. Why have they ever bothered to meddle in elections they can't win?

To use their own words, "for training, experience," and to keep a certain amount of their propaganda before the voters.

69. They don't think they could put Communism over here by peaceful ballot, do they?

Says William Z. Foster, present head of the Party in this country:

There must be no illusions about peacefully capturing the state.

70. Well, what's the REAL Communist program for capturing our Government?

It starts with spying and infiltration of the sort now going on. Then confusion and chaos caused by sudden paralysis of our communications, transportation, money system and law enforcement.

Finally, direct seizure of power.

Communists have spent the last fifteen years hiding their key men in our Army, Navy, diplomatic corps, treasury, and other control points of Government.

71. How do you know they're there?

Ten years of this committee's records, plus the convictions and indictments obtained by the Department of Justice. For an outside check, read the Report of the Canadian Royal Commission, June 27, 1946, on the spy ring caught in Ottawa, Canada.

72. Can you tell something about it?

Yes. Igor Gouzenko, a code clerk in the Russian Embassy there, suddenly walked out one day in September 1945 and handed the Canadian government official Russian spy papers that showed how just ONE group he knew about had stolen U. S. secrets in wartime.

73. Such as?

Samples of atomic bomb explosive, secrets of radar, radio-controlled shell fuses, and other highly secret and important instruments of U. S. fighting power.

74. How did the spies get those?

Some traitors in the United States Government gave them to Russian agents who took them out by way of Canada.

75. Who?

The story is not yet all told. We recommend that you get detailed reports and hearings of this committee, to keep abreast of developments.

76. What?

For instance the Interim Report on Communist Espionage in the United States Government, August 28, 1948; and the Second Report, Soviet Espionage Within the United States Government, December 31, 1948. Write the Government Printing Office for each pamphlet.[4]

77. Can you give some facts here?

Briefly, a former Communist courier, Elizabeth T. Bentley, testified there were two spy groups in the Government with which she worked between 1941 and 1944—The Silvermaster group and Perlo group. Another former Communist agent, Whittaker Chambers, said he had his own apparatus in Government agencies from 1932 to 1938 and that several others were operating at the same time.

78. Did they name names?

Yes. Bentley named 30 Government employees and Chambers named 9 who they testified were in the Communist underground.

When the committee brought the principal subjects before it to ask them about the charges, they refused to answer on grounds they might "incriminate" themselves.

79. Were these people important?

They held top jobs in our Government and some of them held commissions in the United States Army.

80. Is there any proof that Government secrets were really stolen as Chambers has alleged?

Chambers has produced a sheaf of confidential documents which were stolen from our State Department and other agencies. One result—Alger Hiss, former State Department official, has been indicted for perjury by a Federal Grand Jury. The Grand Jury investigation of espionage in our Government is still going on.[5]

81. How serious is this theft of documents?

Well, just consider.

Not only did Russia get secret U. S. military and diplomatic information from the documents—she also had the key to our code system

---

[4] Interim Report, 10c each; Second Report, 25c each; at Superintendent of Documents, Government Printing Office, Washington, D. C.
[5] The first trial of Alger Hiss resulted in a hung jury by a vote of 8 to 4 for conviction. The second trial has been scheduled for October 1949.

so that she could intercept and understand all other secret messages sent by our State Department.

Since Stalin was teamed up with Hitler in this period, the Nazis probably knew our Government secrets, too.

82. What has your committee found out about Communism within our atomic energy program?

Plenty. They have espionage rings which have been operating at least since 1942, using American science and money to inform the Soviet Government of Russia on how to make the atom bomb.

83. Did they tell the Russians the "secret" of the bomb?

Only the Russians and their spies know how much actually got abroad.

For a more detailed idea of what this committee has learned to date about this matter, read the committee's "Report on Soviet Espionage Activities in Connection with the Atom Bomb," September 28, 1948, available at the Government Printing Office.

84. What are some of the things it shows?

For instance, Arthur Adams, who has been a Communist revolutionary since 1905, penetrated to the heart of the electronics industry which was supplying information to our wartime atom bomb developments. He was in physical contact with Clarence Hiskey and other atomic scientists on the famous "Manhattan Project."

In 1944, agents of the Manhattan District searched his rooms and there found "highly secret information" regarding the atomic bomb plant at Oak Ridge, Tenn., and other vitally important matters.

85. Is that all your report shows?

By no means. The report traces out in detail exactly how Adams and other agents were brought into the atomic energy program, who did the job, when, where and how, and in all lists a score of people who were in one way or another, at one time or another, used to further the interests of the Soviet Government against the welfare of the United States.

86. Who besides your committee has anything to say about this?

On September 10, 1948, Gen. Leslie R. Groves, former head of the Manhattan District, testified:

I have no hesitancy in saying that there was continued and persistent and well-organized espionage against the United States, and particularly against the atom bomb project, by a foreign power with which we were not at war, and its misguided and traitorous domestic sympathizers or perhaps stooges would be a better word. * * *

87. *And that sort of character has been living off my tax money?*

Has been, still is, and still will be, until **YOU** force every Communist out of power.

88. *How?*

Detection. Exposure. Prosecution.

89. *Are any of these being done?*

Not very well, even though Congress has been wrestling with the problem now for ten years.

90. *What's the story?*

On May 10, 1938, the House set this Committee on Un-American Activities to work. Since then, 25,000 pages of public and executive testimony have been taken. It has made 50 reports to the House, which include recommendations for new laws.

91. *What's all this cost the taxpayer?*

The Committee's total appropriations to date have been $1,050,000.

92. *Has Congress followed the Committee's suggestions?*

In 1939, Congress forbade federal employees to be members of any group advocating the overthrow of the Constitution.

In 1941, it strengthened that law by refusing pay to any person proved a member of any such group.

It has passed further laws giving the various executive agencies special powers and money to get rid of subversives.

93. *Any results?*

So little that in July 1946 a House Civil Service subcommittee urged a complete overhaul of security measures in the executive branch.

On November 25, 1946, the President set up a commission to deal with employee loyalty. For two years since, an elaborate screening program has been under way.

94. What has THAT cost?

Funds appropriated by Congress for this screening program in the 1948 fiscal year totaled $11,000,000. For the 1949 fiscal year, $6,606,000.

95. How does it work?

This gives you an idea. A federal employee who gets a job goes right to work before his loyalty to our Government is ever established.

It doesn't matter whether he is hired for a minor clerkship or a "sensitive" job of importance to national security, he still can be on the payroll for at least 120 days before the various checkups can determine whether he is a safe risk.

96. Well, is it keeping down the risk?

This committee feels the Communists have such deep-laid lines into the federal departments that the present security system is a feeble defense.

97. What do you recommend?

In the second session, the 80th Congress, this committee brought out a bill, known popularly as the Mundt-Nixon bill. This contains the principles of law we feel necessary, still.

98. What are these?

A penalty of as much as ten years in jail and a $10,000 fine for anybody trying to set up a foreign-directed dictatorship in this country.

Registration of Communists and their organizations as foreign agents.

No passports for Communists.

Tougher rules to keep Communists out of our Government.

99. How far did it get?

Passed the House 319 to 58. Died in the Senate.

100. What next?

That's up to the 81st Congress and you.[6]

---

[6] New Communist control bills have been introduced during the 81st Congress by various Members of the House and Senate. The Mundt-Nixon bill has been reintroduced.

SPOTLIGHT ON SPIES

Conditions in America present the most fertile soil for Soviet espionage.

—VICTOR KRAVCHENKO,
Former Soviet official.

The Communist Party is like a submerged submarine; the part that you see above water is the periscope, but the part underneath is the real Communist organization; that is the conspiratorial apparatus.

—J. PETERS,
Russian head of a Communist spy ring in the U. S. A.

Spotlight On Spies

This is the story of Communist spying in the United States. But don't look for the names of spies. We don't name them.

What we are trying to do is to show you that there IS such a thing as a Soviet spy system in our country, what it is after, how it works, and what it has succeeded in doing so far. It is the right and duty of every American citizen to know these facts.

The information we are setting before you is based on many long hours of investigation by the staff of the Committee on Un-American Activities and many hundreds of pages of testimony by witnesses, some of them former spies for the Soviet Union in the United States.

What is a spy?

A person employed by or in the service of a foreign government, either with or without pay, to secure information considered vital to the waging of a shooting or economic war against another country.

Will you find them in America?

Yes.

Are all spies in America citizens of foreign countries?

No. Many American citizens have been recruited in the service of other governments.

What governments have spied on us in the past?

The Germans during World Wars I and II had agents in this country. Many of these were caught and convicted.

The Russian Government has had spies in the United States since 1922, but their operations were not exposed until recently.

Why do the Russians continue to spy on us?

The aim of the rulers of Russia is to take over the United States along with the rest of the world. Her spies are here to pave the way for a Soviet America.

How do Soviet leaders think we can be taken over?

By a revolt led by Communists in this country during some kind of national economic crisis, or through an armed attack.

How big is the Soviet spy ring here?

Naturally, we can never know the exact size, but former ringleaders have confessed there are thousands of Russian agents, as well as many more thousands of Americans, who are selling us down the river.

In fact, we are the NUMBER ONE target of Russia's spy effort.

Does this constitute a dangerous situation?

To answer this it is only necessary to quote the testimony of the Honorable J. Edgar Hoover, Director of the Federal Bureau of Investigation, before this Committee, which was that "The Communist Party of the United States is a fifth column if there ever was one." He also said there are 74,000 Communist Party members in the United States, but, "What is important is the claim of the Communists themselves that for every Party member there are 10 others ready, willing, and able to do the Party's work.

This means that at a time of national crisis, the United States would have nearly 825,000 persons who are either spies, traitors, or saboteurs working against us from within.

Can our country afford this?

Why is the United States the number one target of the Soviet spy system?

Well, the United States is the most powerful and advanced nation on the earth today. Its scientific and technical success is matched by none. Russia wants the industrial capacity of the United States.

Just what are Soviet spies after?

Everything there is to know about the United States.

What do they want most?

Production secrets of the atom bomb.

What about other military defenses?

They want to know everything about them, too.

The Committee has uncovered recent secret orders from abroad to spy leaders in the United States listing twenty-odd categories of information they want on the armed strength of this country.

These include:

Aviation:
  Total number of aircraft formations; combat and numerical strength of units
  Distribution of base and alternate airfields, their technical equipment and characteristics
  Civilian aviation
  New types of planes
  New technical inventions in the aviation field, in detail, whether applicable in the air or on the ground
  Radar
  Robot planes

Ground troops:
  Infantry—numerical strength, distribution, organization, combat manuals, firing power, training status, morale, combat status, officers' staff

Artillery and armored troops, particularly production, application of V-1 and V-2

Navy:
  General description of the naval fleet and organization
  Principal Navy bases and descriptions

Chemical units:
  Organization and distribution
  New inventions in chemical warfare

Are the spies after diplomatic secrets?

Yes, they want American plans for dealing with Russia and other nations.

Also any secret or open agreements which America might have with other countries. Even the foreign policy ideas of individual politicians must be furnished by the spies.

What about our industry?

Soviet Russia keeps a close watch on it. Here are some of the things Communist spies have to report on, according to secret spy orders in the hands of the Committee on Un-American Activities:

  Principal branches of industry, especially war industry; the production of various enterprises and branches of industry
  Location of industry, especially war industries
  Status of various firms, their productive capacity, type of production, number employed
  Construction of new industrial plants, especially war plants
  Technical innovations in industry
  Work of engineers, research institutions, and laboratories

Any other economic facts?

Yes. For instance, everything about our natural resources and raw materials—with the stress on those having possible military value.

Is this all?

No. As we said, they want to know EVERYTHING about the United States.

But we don't make any secret of some of the things Russia wants, do we?

No. But Soviet Russia wants more than we are willing to give.

Well, America wouldn't let spies obtain our REAL secrets, would she?

Not intentionally, but an ex-Soviet spy told this Committee that this country is the easiest in the world for spies to work in and obtain secret information.

Why is this?

Because of the number of Soviet sympathizers whose jobs put them in a position to get secret information.

Because of the naive attitude of many Americans about the Communist danger.

Who runs the Communist spy system in America?

Russian Communists who are trained in espionage and sent over here to direct the spy work on the spot.

Are they the real bosses?

No. They are the "foremen." They see that American spies carry out Soviet orders for secret information and that the secret information gets back to Russia.

The REAL boss is the Soviet Government.

How do they get into this country?

One class of Russian spy leaders gets in on fake travel papers and quickly drops out of sight. Only trusted Communist lieutenants ever are in close contact with them. Even they know them only by some simple name such as "Al," "Carl," "Bill," or "Jack."

116

How else do Russian agents get in?

Some are sent here as military, political, or as other official representatives of the Soviet Government. They may be attached to the Soviet Embassy in Washington, D. C., or the United Nations headquarters in New York.

Still others are disguised as "commercial agents" for the Soviet Union. They have quietly carried on their spy work in such commercial firms as "World Tourists" and "Amtorg Trading Company" in New York City.

Even those officials who are not working with organized spy rings are ordered to collect what information they can while in the United States.

How could the United Nations be used?

An outstanding example is the former Russian military attaché in Canada, who was exposed as the head of a huge spy ring working against the Canadian Government. He was forced to leave Canada, but he later was admitted to the United States as a UN representative for the Soviet Union.

Or take the case of the Russian "engineer" stationed at UN headquarters in New York who was arrested by the FBI on March 4, 1949, with an American employee of our own Government and charged with spying.

Do these Russian spy agents work in one big ring?

No. They run a lot of separate spy rings. Each agent and his ring are kept in the dark about the work of the other rings.

Who serve as the actual thieves for these spy rings?

Self-styled "loyal" AMERICANS, believe it or not.

You mean an American would actually betray his own country to help Soviet Russia?

We have confessions to prove it.

But what kind of people can they be?

Treasonable creatures who enjoy the privileges of American citizenship and talk loudly about their loyalty, but all the time are REALLY loyal only to Russia.

This boils down to Communist Party members and their sympathizers.

Are all Communists spies?

Yes, in one sense, for it is every Communist's duty to report anything he learns that might help the Soviet Union.

But in the organized spy rings, whose target includes America's top secrets, only carefully selected Communists and sympathizers are used.

How are American Communists recruited for spy rings?

First of all, every Communist's record is filed in Moscow. When Soviet leaders notice an American Communist who seems particularly suitable for spy work or is in a good spot to learn American secrets, or render some other service, he is marked for the role of a spy.

Sometimes American leaders recommend a comrade for the work, and Moscow checks his record and gives the okay.

What kind of records does Moscow keep?

Everything about a person. For instance, his job, education, family, acquaintances, finances, politics, criminal record, if any, and personal habits. Even such personal things as his ability to hold liquor. Some of this information can be used as a club over the individual if he threatens to break.

Are American Communists trained in spy work?

Not in any formal way. All Party work involves secret, underhanded actions so a seasoned Communist could step right into spy work when ordered.

.If inexperienced Communists are in a spot to help the spy rings, they might be given "special treatment."

What is this "special treatment"?

They are invited to join small Communist "study groups" which to outsiders appear to be harmless social gatherings or discussion groups.

Actually, these gatherings are used to teach the "students" blind loyalty to the Soviet Union and to get them into a conspiratorial frame of mind against the American Government.

Then what?

Communist spy agents get progress reports on the "students" and when it looks as though they are ready to do anything for the Soviet Union, the agents will take them into the spy rings.

Do these Americans betray their country for money?

Not all the time. Sometimes when an American Communist enters a spy ring, he is shocked if money is offered to him.

Russian agents have had to trick some American agents into taking rewards.

What's back of these rewards?

Useful as blackmail in case a spy gets scared and wants to quit. For that reason, spies who receive money are forced to sign receipts which are sent to Moscow.

How can spies be tricked into taking money?

Usually by giving them lump sums of money for "expenses."

Then there are "good will" presents such as expensive rugs, which four American spies in high U. S. Government jobs received from the Soviet Government.

Is an American ever "forced" into a spy ring?

Sometimes. We know of an American in our War Department who was scared into stealing secrets because the Russians threatened to harm his relatives in Russia.

Russian agents make a special effort to find out and use Americans with close relatives in the Soviet Union.

Would anyone but a fool be willing to spy for Russia?

No. But you'll find "fools" in pretty HIGH places.

Soviet spy rings contain well-educated and able Americans who are looked up to by their fellow men. They may be scientists, lawyers, professors, writers, Government career workers, and even successful businessmen who have been filled with Communist poison.

Do these spies really know what they're doing?

Wouldn't you?

Well, just how does a spy ring operate?

Picture a production line. At one end, we have the American spy, who is stealing material Russia is interested in. Next, we have the "go-between" who receives the material from the spy and passes it on to the Russian boss. Then it's headed for Russia.

Can you give more details?

Let's take it step by step.

Suppose the American spy works in the War Department. He keeps his eyes and ears open for every bit of information he can learn. He goes out of his way to be friendly with others who might know something of value. He snoops in the files and records when no one is looking. He learns a lot this way, because no one knows he is a spy.

What happens then?

Committee investigations have shown that the spy turns his information over to a "go-between" or "courier." Sometimes he tells the courier what he has heard; sometimes he gives him notes, and copies of letters or other papers revealing secret plans. Sometimes he even steals original records from the Government files and turns them over to the courier.

Just who is this "courier"?

A trusted American Communist who acts as messenger for a Russian spy boss. This courier picks up information gathered by American spies and passes on to them orders from the Russian agent in charge.

If the Russian had to personally contact all his spies, he would arouse suspicion.

How does the spy get information to the courier?

They make a date to meet—maybe at a restaurant, a drug store, or the home of a Communist. Maybe even in a park or on a street corner. There the spy turns over his material and finds out if the Russians want any particular job done. The spy knows the courier only by some alias such as "Carl" or "Helen."

Is this the only way?

No. The spy can mail information to an address of a trusted Communist, where the courier will pick it up.

What's the next step?

Well, the courier has to get the stuff to a Russian agent. One ex-courier told us he would sometimes have a trusted photographer make tiny pictures (known as microfilm) of the secret information so that it could be delivered less conspicuously.

120

In the case of original documents that were stolen, they had to be photographed right away so the spy could put them back in the files before they were missed.

How does the courier carry this stolen booty?

The most obvious ways, in the cases we know of.

A brief case, or, if the courier is a woman, a large purse, knitting bag, or shopping bag.

And then?

The courier furtively hands over his haul to a Russian agent whose job is to get it to Russia.

How DOES it get there?

There are plenty of tricky ways. For instance:

Short-wave radio, if it's "hot" news

Diplomatic mail pouches from Soviet Government officials here

Russian officials who travel back and forth on United Nations and other business

Russian undercover agents traveling on false passports

Communist businessmen whose custom it is to take business trips abroad

Communist seamen

How can a seaman help?

Easy. No one pays any attention to his traveling because it's his livelihood. Even if his ship doesn't touch Russia, he can still deliver secret messages to Communists in other countries, who will see that they reach Moscow. Sometimes these people are not really seamen at all, but Communist agents with fake seamen's papers.

What precautions are taken in sending stolen material?

Radio messages are sent in code.

Official Russian mail cannot be opened by anyone.

And for Russian undercover agents and Communist seamen who serve as couriers, there are countless clever ways to hide secret information.

Can you name some of these?

The back is removed from a dime-store pocket mirror, tiny photographs of secret material are inserted against the glass, and the back is then replaced.

How else?

Tiny photographic films, containing secret messages, are soaked in a solution to make them flexible as cloth. Then this soft film is tightly rolled up, put into a small cylinder, and inserted into a tube of toothpaste.

Any other methods?

Sometimes the film is softened in the same way and cut up and sewed inside the lining of neckties.

Messages have also been placed in hollow parts of toys and in the hollow handles of safety razors.

What happens when the information gets to Russia?

The Russians sort out the information which is pouring in. Bits of information from separate American spy rings are pieced together. If something is missing to make a complete picture of some American project, orders go back to the spy rings to concentrate on that particular point.

Don't spies ever duplicate each other's work?

All the time. Because, besides carrying out special orders, American spies pick up any and all information they can lay their hands on. Furthermore, each spy ring in America works independently of the others.

The screening process takes place in Russia.

Isn't this a costly operation?

Sure. But it's so important to the Soviet Union that money is no object. Russian agents are free-handed in their offers of "gifts" to American spies. They have handed out as much as two thousand dollars at a time.

Where does the money come from?

The Soviet Government, and sometimes wealthy American Communists or sympathizers.

Where does the Communist Party of the United States fit into the scheme?

It's a separate organization from the huge spy network although the network draws upon the Party for spies and couriers and any other help it may need.

But wouldn't spies who are Party workers be easy to spot?

No. For it is Party policy to give "super" secret membership to certain classes of people such as students, scientists, teachers, office workers, administrative, and Government workers.

Other Party members are kept from knowing these people are in the Party. They never hold Party membership cards or attend regular Party meetings. In fact, they're not allowed even to discuss their real political views with anybody.

So what job a Communist holds has a lot to do with his selection for spy work?

Yes, if he's in a position to steal information for the Russians. And a file clerk can be as useful as an executive.

But a highly placed Communist is valuable in still another way—he can use his influence to get other Communists into jobs involving secret information.

What about spies in our Government?

Two former couriers for spies within our Government told your Committee how they worked.

One courier headed a ring of spies who were in such Federal agencies as the War, State, Navy, Justice, Treasury, Labor, Agriculture, and Commerce Departments. The other received information from high Government officials.

The couriers said other spy rings operated at the same time in our Government.

Were the spies in spots where they could steal secrets?

Several spies had such important jobs that it was their duty to handle confidential State Department papers.

Several others actually worked within one of our Government's own intelligence groups during the war. Others within the armed forces.

Did they succeed in stealing information?

Your Committee has copies of more than 60 secret State Department papers—dealing with American diplomatic relations with other countries—which were stolen by a spy. We can't tell you what some of them say because even now it would endanger the safety of our country.

Yet this was just the result of one spy's work in one week. THINK WHAT THE TOTAL OUTPUT MUST BE.

Are spies after our Government secrets RIGHT NOW?

You can be sure of it.

Where would you find spies in industry?

Well, we told you they wanted to know everything about our industry.

But, particularly watch for them in:

Atomic plants	Steel firms
Aviation companies	Maritime industries
Submarine companies	Chemical and other research institutions
Munitions works	Communications
Transportation	Oil and mining industries

Why these particularly?

Important from a war angle.

What has happened in the atomic field?

Since the atom bomb is Russia's chief worry right now, she has several spy rings concentrating on that alone.

Where are these atomic spies?

Your Committee has shown that they have penetrated right to the very heart of our atomic work. Some agents working for the Communists have contacted scientists working in the most secret branches of atomic research.

Then haven't they made away with some of our atomic secrets?

We KNOW they have, but just how much of the entire formula of the bomb is unknown.

How about aviation?

We know of a Russian agent, skilled in aviation, who, with the help of other spies, collected a huge store of confidential aviation data. It contained photographs, blueprints, and notes which were personally flown to Moscow by the chairman of the then active Soviet Purchasing Commission.

Two spies were decorated by the Soviet Government for this.

And the submarine field?

Blueprints, photographs, and technical descriptions have been sneaked out of American submarine companies by spies and sent to Moscow.

In several cases, Russian agents directing the work were Soviet naval captains pretending to be civilians with entirely different interests.

Can you give an example in the steel industry?

Yes. An American scientist held a top research job with one of our biggest steel companies. He was a spy and, every week or two, he flew half way across the country to turn over information to a Russian spy agent.

What is the interest in steel?

New formulas for making it, for one thing. The amount of steel produced is another.

What Communists in industry CAN be trusted?

None, when you get right down to it. It's every Communist's duty, even as a mechanic or office worker, to pick up any information around the plant he can lay hands on. Though he may not act under an organized spy ring, he can often turn up information which Moscow wants.

This applies to Communists in the Government and anywhere else, too.

How would secrets from Communists outside a spy ring get to Russia?

Here's one example:

A Communist in a submarine-building plant regularly gave information he gathered about the plant to the Communist Party organizer in his district. The organizer sent it on to national Communist Party headquarters which in turn handed it over to a Russian spy.

Any other way?

Communist union officials could also send through the channels described above any important material collected by a Communist worker.

Just how successful is the Soviet spy system in America?

An Army general said that when this country is compared with Canada you get some idea of the success because Russian spies in Canada obtained an enormous amount of information.

Why can we be sure of this?

Because the spies have been with us for close to 30 years and America is only beginning to wake up to the fact that there are such things as Soviet spies.

Until lately, Communists even succeeded in getting Government positions no matter how secret the work.

All this is pretty serious, isn't it?

Very, very serious.

But in the case of much important information, Russian agents haven't had to steal it. We have GIVEN it away.

What do you mean?

For one thing, we have tried to be friendly to Russia and as a result Russian officials have been able to collect a lot of our industrial and military inventions just by buying patents for the inventions from our Government Patent Office. This is done right out in the open with our permission.

Has this been done on a large scale?

So large that Russia has practically EVERY American patent dealing with industrial, chemical, and military inventions which have been released to the public. This runs into the hundreds of thousands.

What do these patents cover?

Here are a few of the types bought by Russia:

Bomb-sight	Bomb-dropping device
Military tank	Helicopter
Airplane	Mine sweeper
Ship control	Ammunition
Bullet-resisting armor	

But won't Russia do the same for us?

Russia has refused to give out a single one of her patents since 1927.

What else have we GIVEN away?

During the war, because they were our allies, Russian visitors were invited to inspect our country and its defense industries. One of the results was that the Russians betrayed our friendship and printed a thick book which can easily be used as a handbook for bombing and sabotage against the United States.

What does the book show?

In pictures, maps, and words, the location and lay-outs of our Nation's large power dams and power plants, aircraft and auto factories, plants dealing with metals, bridges, railroads, and important communications.

Is America doing anything to protect herself from Soviet spies?

Yes. The world's finest investigative agency is on the job—the FBI. It is aided by Military and Naval Intelligence.

Isn't this enough?

Far from it. Every patriotic American must be on the alert and report all suspicious activities brought to his or her attention to either the Federal Bureau of Investigation, the Army or Navy Intelligence services, local police departments, and/or the Committee on Un-American Activities.

This is particularly important since the spy network is growing bigger because of new sources for spies.

What are these new sources?

New Communist governments such as Poland, Hungary, Czechoslovakia, Bulgaria, and Albania.

How is this of help to Russia?

These countries send Communists over here to represent them in their embassies and legations, in the United Nations, and on other missions.

These Communists are just as willing to spy for Russia as a Russian Communist. For all Communists everywhere are loyal to the Soviet Union.

Is there any proof?

The former top military officer of a Russian satellite embassy, in Washington, D. C., got disgusted with the Communists and exposed a spy ring working from his embassy.

What did he confess?

He said the spy ring he knew about in America was Nation-wide and looking for scientific, political, and industrial information about our country.

He said the ring was directed from the Russian Embassy in Washington and information collected sent out in diplomatic mail pouches to Russia by way of another country.

What else did he say?

That other spy rings could be found here in the embassies and legations of all Balkan countries under control of Russia.

When necessary, the United Nations was also used as a hide-out for these Balkan Communist spies.

What should we do about the Soviet spy system in America?

Redouble our efforts to root out the spies and send them to jail or to Russia.

Since American Communists are so necessary to the Soviet spy rings, we must also concentrate on exposing every one of them, wherever they may be found.

New laws are needed, too.

What kind of laws?

Laws that will give tougher penalties to anyone stealing secret information for Russia, whether in peace or in war.

Laws that will clamp down on the activities of Russian agents in this country and of American Communists in foreign countries. Any other laws that will help us stamp out the spy network, as well as Communist cells.

Is it too late to start now?

Of course not. Spying is a never-ending business with the Russians.

New secrets are being born every day as American science and industry progress.

What we do NOW to stop the spies and Communists means a lot to the future safety of our country.

What is the Committee on Un-American Activities doing about all this?

Your Committee's job is to show the American people what the Communists are up to, and suggest any new laws needed to deal with them.

The Committee is doing everything it can to run down the Communist spy rings in this country and has already succeeded in exposing many of the spies. It has also offered a new law to Congress and is studying still others—all aimed at curbing the Communist spy business.

What can I do to help?

Do some deep thinking about what the Soviet spy system and the American Communist mean to the safety of our country.

Then let your Government and your Congress know that you want to see REAL ACTION to rid our country of these menaces.

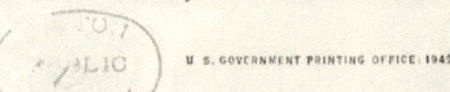

U. S. GOVERNMENT PRINTING OFFICE: 1949

www.ingramcontent.com/pod-product-compliance
Lightning Source LLC
Chambersburg PA
CBHW020320290526
45785CB00007B/2863